Money Messages

Get Out of the Red and Into the Green
Emotional and Financial Freedom to
Transform Your Life

Jody Robinson

with Karen Putz

Jody Robinson

Ka Putz

Money Messages: Get Out of the Red and Into the Green, Emotional and Financial Freedom to Transform Your Life

ISBN: 978-1-7344089-0-4

Library of Congress Control Number: 2019920863

Also available in eBook and Audio book formats

Editor: Tyler Tichelaar, Superior Book Productions

Cover Art: Catherine Borzym, Kiwi Avenue

Interior and Cover Layout: Larry Alexander, Superior Book Productions

For information about special discounts for bulk purchases, please contact Robinson Publications: moneymessage@outlook.com

To my son

Acknowledgments

WITHOUT KAREN PUTZ, THIS BOOK would not be possible. I have met many amazing women in my life, and Karen is one of those mindset life changers. After becoming deaf as a teen from a fall while barefoot waterskiing, Karen spent several years trying to find her path. At the age of forty-four, she returned to the sport and rediscovered her passion.

Karen decided to study everything she could about "passion" and the meaning behind the word. Today, not only has she been backwards barefoot waterskiing in waters known to have alligators (her greatest fear), but she has helped publish or write more than ten books—she recently made the Amazon bestsellers' list in Personal Success and Spirituality with her book Unwrapping Your Passion—next to another of my favorite authors, Wayne Dyer. Karen also paints, speaks all over the world about the topic of passion, and runs The Passion School, helping other people live their passions.

Thank you to my business coach, life coach, and counselor, Rima. You saved my life and my business and have been instrumental in guiding me to live my most authentic life in my work and my family.

I am grateful to my Aunt Barb, who never gave up on me, even at the lowest points in my life, when I wasn't sure about my life's purpose. You have been a mom to me, a friend, and a cohort in mischief. We've road-tripped across the state to research our genealogy (during which time we almost killed each other, but we still love each other), shared a few bottles of wine, and lifted each other up when things got tough.

Cherie, my sister, you are the strongest person I know. I am so proud of you, and you've taught me so much about being a good mom and not giving up in the face of adversity.

And Mom and Dad, I hope you get to see that your daughter turned out okay, and that you are proud of me.

To my husband, John, my rock, my love, and my big, adorable, manly man. You've had my back during my crazy career and wild ideas—and you have been my biggest cheerleader. You stood up for me when I was weak, and you stood beside me when I was strong. You never stood in front of me and made me feel small. Thanks for all the nights cooking together or creating culinary masterpieces for my son and me, and for listening to me and being my best friend. I hope we laugh and love together for many, many years to come.

And finally, to my son. Mr. Nu, you are my reason for being. Until you were born, I never knew how much I could love another person. I hope you grow up with positivity, personal growth, and all the wonderful things life has to offer. And when you hit those bumps in the road, know that I am always there with you, helping you through and sending my love. I am writing this book so you can always keep a part of me with you. You are amazing, creative, and so, so smart. You can do anything you set your mind to—and never let anyone tell you differently!

Contents

INTRODUCTION... 1

PART I: UNDERSTANDING MONEY MESSAGES.......................... 9

Chapter 1: Taking Charge of Your Destiny............................ 11

Chapter 2: Where Do You Want to Take Your Boat? 17

Chapter 3: The Purpose of Money.. 21

Chapter 4: Hold Fast to Your Dreams 27

Chapter 5: Conscious Money Choices 43

Chapter 6: Money Stories... 49

Chapter 7: Turning Points: My Money Story 59

PART II: REWRITING YOUR MONEY MESSAGES........................ 73

Chapter 8: Understanding Your Money Messages 75

Chapter 9: Your Circumstances and Your Choices 91

Chapter 10: Love and Money Messages:
Finding Financial Compatibility.. 109

Chapter 11: Mary Beth Franklin,
the 2 A.M. Epiphany, and Passion....................................... 117

Chapter 12: Flip the Script 125

PART III: INVESTING IN YOU.. 135

Chapter 13: Money Messages and Your Investing Behavior 137

Chapter 14: Buckets: Paying Off Debt.................................. 145

Chapter 15: Creating Your Plan B 153

Chapter 16: The Golden Years: Or Are They?....................... 159

Chapter 17: Tying It All Together: What's Next?................... 171

A Final Note... 177

BONUS SECTION:
ADDITIONAL MONEY MESSAGE TOOLS 181

Your Next Amazing Journey in Reading............................... 183

TED Talks 185

How to Find a Financial Advisor.. 187

Savvy Money-Saving Food Prep Tips
from Jody and Her Grandma... 195

ABOUT THE AUTHORS 199

INTRODUCTION

"Maybe the journey isn't so much about becoming anything. Maybe it's about un-becoming everything that isn't really you so you can be who you were meant to be in the first place."

— Paul Coelho, Brazilian lyricist, novelist, and self-proclaimed hippie

M*Y SON, ON THE BRINK* of being a teenager, recently asked me, "Mom, am I good enough?"

That question broke my heart because I know we all ask ourselves that question at some point.

"Good enough for what? We are all good enough for whatever we want to be," I told him.

You, my reader, are also good enough to do what you put your mind to. We are all children of this world, and we need to be kind and hold each other, and ourselves, as special and worth being held in respect and love. I want *you* to find a place of peace, happiness, and financial freedom from debt and constant worry.

Mel Robbins, in her TEDxSF talk about "How to Stop Screwing Yourself Over," tells us we have a 1:400,000,000,000 chance of being born with the DNA structure we have. That is 400 trillion! That means there's literally no one like you. We are each special, and our path is unique to us. Comparing ourselves to anyone else or letting anyone else compare us is simply irrelevant.

I never could have anticipated the twists and turns it took to get me here today, in front of this computer, sharing with you about money and life fulfillment. I grew up as an idealistic, grunge-hippy chick, detesting just about everything about materialism. I was a small-town girl in the Great Plains; wandering in God's country was my pastime. From the Bible, I learned materialistic pursuits were evil and punishable by judgment and eternal damnation. I was a little wild child, preferring mud pies and twigs in my hair to a makeup table or dress clothes. I remember countless hours weeding beside my mother or helping her to can the fruits of our labor. Today, gardening is still my escape, my meditation, and my home.

Ironically, I've spent the better portion of the last two decades devoted to either working in the front of an investment office, having conversations with nervous clients before they go to meet with a financial advisor, or later, sitting in the chair as *the* financial advisor. Sometimes it's fun; sometimes it's frustrating.

I do keep a box of tissues handy. We laugh, we think, and sometimes, we shed tears together. Money is a sensitive topic. Talking about our power and the ability to procure the lifestyle we desire can be an intimate experience, and for some, a difficult or even impossible conversation. With courage and faith in ourselves, we can step forward to achieve more than we ever thought possible!

My son has watched me work long hours serving clients. For most of his young years, he was in daycare or with babysitters. Later, when I was a divorced parent, he was sometimes in the next room, playing games while I met clients or Rotarians. God bless him, he's always taken an interest in his mommy's career and volunteerism.

I fashion myself a humanitarian and financial counselor. Technically speaking, I am a fiduciary, certified Accredited Wealth Management Advisor from the College for Financial Planning and a partner at a wealth management firm. I enjoy teaching kids and adults about leadership and how to overcome adversity in finances.

At the beginning of my career, I followed my training and did the typical things a financial advisor would say or do. But as time went on, life happened, and I realized there were no cookie-cutter answers—and no holy grail of investing or financial planning. I often detest the "instruction" that is fed to me in my continuing education, but I understand it is a necessary evil. Every class has some good pointers I try to pay attention to and take with me, and I continue to pursue my academic studies, mostly because I am required to as part of my job.

I would much rather focus on psychology and mental health because I find the self-study I have done in these areas much more applicable and helpful in assisting my clients to move to a better lifestyle and mindset with money. I love seeing the progress my clients make when they tap into their power. You can math me to death, but that isn't going to help my client sitting across from me, asking me how to use money to live a better life.

My son often asks me questions on *what* I do to help people and why I'm so passionate about it. *What* I do is not easily put into a title or a sentence, but the closest thing I can say is: *I help people work on their Money Messages (perceptions of money) so they can live the best life possible. I help people find wealth in purpose, and purpose assigned to their wealth.*

Sometimes that work entails helping them work through a Money Mindset that is blocking them from moving forward financially. For example, a belief that "Money is the root of all evil" may stop a person from saving money. I help them understand that money is not evil, but rather, it is a tool they can use to take care of their family, and if they wish, benefit their community. Once they understand that, they can make healthy financial decisions.

Now that my son is close to adulthood, this book is also a gift for him to read unfiltered, to hopefully catch him up on any lessons I may not have shared with him as a child.

Lessons like:

- What does it take to be fulfilled?

- How does someone get "good" with money?

- What is "success"?

- What are the mindset and Money Messages of self-made wealthy, healthy, and happy people?

- How can we avoid the mistakes other people make in spending, saving, and investing?

Before we go further, I want you to stop and think about those lessons. Perhaps you haven't learned them yet, but you may have some thoughts upon them. In the spaces below, please write your thoughts on those lessons.

REFLECTION AND SOUL SEARCH

What does it take to be fulfilled?

_____

_____

_____

_____

How does someone get "good" with money?

_____

_____

_____

What is "success"?

_____

_____

_____

What are some of the mindset and Money Messages of self-made wealthy, healthy, and happy people?

_____

_____

_____

How can we avoid the mistakes other people make in spending, saving, and investing?

_____

_____

_____

They don't teach this in schools!

That's one of the biggest complaints I hear from my clients who have children or grandchildren. When I recently discussed this book with a real estate agent, he said to me, "There are so many *adults* who need to learn the valuable lessons of financial literacy."

But what is "financial literacy"? If you watch the news, you would think the investment and financial world has a serious dissociative identity disorder. What does it mean to be wealthy? Is it owning a yacht, or a quiet place in the woods? Is it having exotic parties and fun times, or is it working with your nose to the grindstone? Is it knowing how to invest and save, or is it being able to spend as much as you can? The media has a very twisted way of presenting "wealth." And then there are the financial experts, with megaphones on TV, promising an easy "how to" for all the money and all the lifestyle you've ever dreamed about. Perhaps you bought the video or audio series, but you still feel a bit out in the cold— disconnected?

When I was twenty-five, I would look at forty and fifty-year olds, thinking they had it all figured out. As I approach fifty, I know I have more figured out than I did at twenty-five, but I am still always learning. I also seriously overestimated the wisdom of fifty-year olds when I was twenty-five. I am sharing with you some of the lessons I have learned, and lessons other people have shared with me along the way, having worked in various capacities in financial services for the last two decades.

This book is simply my humble opinion—to add to the cacophony of voices out there on this much discussed subject. The difference is that I want to focus on you: your heart, your mind, and your ambition to work toward ultimate happiness. Truly, it's not about the money. It's about the Money Messages we have internalized that guide our lives.

For that reason, I've divided this book into three parts. Part I is about understanding what Money Messages are, as well as the purpose of money, and figuring out what you want your money to do for you. Part II is about reflecting on your own personal Money Messages and your circumstances. Discover what messages or circumstances might be holding you back from achieving what you want both financially and in all aspects of your life. Finally, Part III is about investing, budgeting, getting out of debt, making good financial choices, and preparing for retirement. It might be that this section is the reason you bought the book, so you may be tempted to jump to it, but it comes last for a reason. Think about investing like marriage. You may want to be married, but until you understand who you are and who your partner is (in terms of investing, understanding your investing behavior, and the messages you internalized about money) you aren't ready for marriage. So please, take the time to explore your relationship with money before you join those two into a union.

In these pages, I will help you get to the heart of those Money Messages. We'll analyze them, discard the ones that don't work for us, create new, positive Money Messages, and then put them to work in creating financial freedom and happiness.

Are you ready to take control of your Money Messages and live a life free of financial worry and guilt? Are you ready to experience financial freedom?

Then please read on and let your financial freedom journey begin.

PART 1
UNDERSTANDING
MONEY MESSAGES

Chapter 1
Taking Charge of Your Destiny

*"The best day of your life is the day on which you decide
your life is yours. No more hiding, self-sabotage or excuses.
No others to cling to or blame. This moment in time is
yours. The doors of opportunities are endless. A magical
journey has begun—and you understand that you hold the
key to the quality of it."*

— Tara Isis Gerris, Founder of Wild Woman Sisterhood

THE HAPPY PEOPLE I HAVE met in my career may not have the same amount in the bank, but they have one thing in common: They are able to save and spend as they wish, without chasing the Joneses next door or getting in over their heads with credit cards or material overconsumption. They are generally not jealous, and they set their own goals for success, unique to them and no one else. Successful people seem to love what they do in life. That's not to say what successful people do is easy, or that they love it every single moment, but they take satisfaction in performing at a high level in their work.

Good wealth builders are committed, engaged, and dedicated to making their lives better. Wise investors realize you can either compound interest to your advantage, or compound debt to your disadvantage.

It took me a long time to learn this.

I am an avid people watcher. I am fascinated with human behavior—always have been. As eighth graders, my best friend and I documented the body language of our teachers and classmates to determine whether it was congruent to the situation or what the person was saying. Today, I am interested in understanding how people feel about and foster their relationships with money, and how that affects their personal relationships.

When I started my financial career, I was racked with anxiety. My daily challenge at the firm was to convince strangers to buy an investment or work with me. A coworker, who mentored me, told me I had to learn how to "sell." This mentor had a lot of experience in sales and sales training. He gave me an audiobook by Tom Hopkins, a sales training expert known for his bestselling book *Master the Art of Selling*. I listened to Tom Hopkins in the car every day and found his words inspiring. He made "asking the hard questions" into a game. The game was still hard, but more like enjoyable exercise than daily torture. Since I still felt extremely insecure as a salesperson, I went to Tom's "sales boot camp" in Arizona. Tom was my first professional guide into sales—he was a very successful "kickin' it old-school" sales teacher.

From Tom, I learned six lessons that go way beyond sales—they're lessons about living life with a sense of integrity and freedom.

During a break at the boot camp, I shyly approached Tom and thanked him for the seminar. "Come here; let's sit," he replied. He motioned me toward a couch in the lobby. For thirty minutes, we talked. I was able to ask him about his happiness and his life path.

Tom told me the amount of wealth he obtained didn't matter to him by that point, but he found great satisfaction in seeing other people attain success. He took me to meet his team, shuttered off from the participants in what could best be described as a "war room," a strategic hub of activity. I was surprised by the number of people working for him—and what a big team he had to pull together all the pieces of his business. When he introduced me to his staff, I could see the pride he had in his team and their pride to work with him. I never saw his team scurrying about—they moved with seamless precision. I think Tom was trying to teach me something by showing me a "behind the scenes" look at his successful business.

These are the six valuable lessons I learned from my short time with Tom:

1. **Don't take advice from someone more messed up than you.** In other words, be cautious of people doling out advice, and use your critical thinking skills. Just because someone is an "expert," you can't follow them blindly. It is still your unique path.

2. **Find passive income.** Don't live forever on the paycheck to paycheck treadmill. You are worth it to think bigger. Create a plan to move beyond the sixty-hour work weeks with no end in sight and nothing to show for all the hard work. This doesn't mean finding a "get rich quick scheme." It means having the discipline to save money that *works* for you!

3. **Success is the continuous journey toward the achievement of predetermined, worthwhile goals.** Without solid goals, you will simply drift through life.

4. **No matter how "big" you are, try to treat *everyone* with love and respect.** What goes around, comes around.

5. **You can't create something amazing all by yourself.** Build a team by selecting people who can share the same vision you have.

6. **Money alone is not enough for a career goal.** You need a strong "why" to push you forward.

If you are saying to yourself, "I want to live with freedom from monetary slavery," or "I am so tired of being on this materialistic hamster wheel to nowhere," then this book is for you. This book is about *quality* of life and examining the aspects of happy and successful people: entrepreneurs, corporate workers, blue collar, white collar, green thumbs, and white gloves.

Mel Robbins, self-help guru, reminds us that we live in such an amazing time because if we want to research a subject, all we must do is find a book online or at a bookstore. We can ride the draft of other people who have gone before us. However, riding the draft and learning from other successful people is *not* the same as comparing ourselves to or copying someone else.... It is taking the best parts of those around us and seeing how we can apply them to our own lives. Learning from others' success means incorporating, melding, and synergizing what will help us on our own path.

Are you ready to take charge of your destiny?

I'm going to let you in on the first two steps—the most valuable observations I have learned—before you read another word in this book. If you take these first baby steps, you will change the path of your life forever, and your relationship with money going forward:

1. **Take Accountability.** Start today. Right now. You can and will do this, either greatly or poorly. This means no more excuses. Wayne Dyer, one of my favorite life coaches, had an audio series I recommend called *Excuses Begone*. You are the captain of your ship, so you control what direction you take in your life and with your money.

2. **Make New Choices.** If the choices you've been making are not serving you well, it's time to make new choices. When you find areas of your life that need improvement or change, nothing will happen until you decide to make new choices.

To move forward, you are going to create a new mindset (Accountability) and recognize new choices (Actions) you can explore.

Below, complete the Accountability and New Choices activity.

REFLECTION AND SOUL SEARCH

Accountability

Identify five choices you've made that have led you to where you are today.

1. _____
2. _____
3. _____
4. _____
5. _____

New Choices

Identify five new choices that will create a new direction for you:

1. _____
2. _____
3. _____
4. _____
5. _____

*T*HE LATE HUGH O'BRIAN, AN actor and youth leadership advocate, wrote a letter to ambassadors of his youth leadership seminar entitled "The Freedom to Choose."

Over 500,000 students' lives have been transformed by these seminars (including mine). He shared in this letter to us:

I do NOT believe we are all born equal— CREATED equal in the eyes of God, YES—but physical and emotional differences, parental guidance, varying environments, being in the right place at the right time, all play a role in enhancing or limiting an individual's development.

But I DO believe every man and woman, if given the opportunity and encouragement to recognize his or her own potential, regardless of background, has the freedom to choose in our world. Will an individual be a taker or a giver in life? Will that person be satisfied merely to exist, or seek a meaningful purpose? Will he or she dare to dream the impossible dream?

*I believe every person is created as the **steward of his or her own destiny** with great power for a specific purpose: to share with others, through service, a reverence for life in a spirit of love.*

Chapter 2
Where Do You Want to Take Your Boat?

"I am the master of my fate; I am the captain of my soul."
— William Ernest Henley

R ECENTLY, I HAD A CONVERSATION with Nick Tokman, known as "Sunshine," from the show, *The Deadliest Catch*. The reality show, which has aired for fifteen seasons to date on The Discovery Channel, is about the struggles and elements fishermen in Alaska must overcome to make a living in some of the most frigid and dangerous waters in the Bering Sea. Nick was always known for his sunshine-bright, positive attitude in the face of danger. Because Nick is sweet and positive, I must say I feel he got bossed around a lot on the show. But he is a strong man. He held his own quite well in the face of not only bad weather, but sometimes bad attitudes around him.

For many years, Nick was passionate about fishing, but as the show went on, he began to realize he wanted a change.

"I love fishing," Nick told me, "but then it started becoming like, I don't know if this is for me anymore. That's okay that what we do changes over time. And it helps us evolve as a people. I think for me, going up to Alaska was to help me find myself, test myself, see what I was capable of. And then I started speaking. I didn't know why I was so passionate about it, but I loved it. I kept doing it more and more. I was just doing it for fun at first, and eventually I knew—*this is what I want to do for my job.*"

Nick decided to change the path of his life and left the show. He took accountability not only for his career path, but today, he tracks and holds himself accountable in how he lives, what he eats, and when/how much he sleeps. He made himself accountable for his physical and mental health—exercising even when he's on the road and taking care of his mental health by reading books to inspire him and help him perform at his highest level of energy. Today, Nick trains people of all ages on positivity in the face of adversity. He enjoys speaking to schools as well as training corporate leaders. One of the main subjects he discusses is taking accountability to set and achieve goals.

> *Other people can try to guide, boss, or help you steer your boat, but ultimately, you make the decision on where to take your boat.*

There is a whole branch of study in psychotherapy that William Glasser, MD, has coined "Choice Theory." The idea behind this theory is simple: We have the power to control our own thoughts and decisions and the limited ability to influence others.

I would love to tell people what to do and then have them just magically do it and be happy and successful, but life doesn't work that way. Every person's path is unique, so what's right for one person is not right for all. I believe our stories do have power to help others see what is possible. In this book, I will share stories from people of various ages and a variety of backgrounds. I'll also share some of my own stories, both regarding my journeys in life and my journeys with money. As you read through the stories, I encourage you to internalize the stories that will help you. If you are willing to *take responsibility, make new choices, and hold yourself accountable for your choices and your actions*, the information in this book can help guide you. Not only will you learn how to prosper, but you will become a different person in the process.

REFLECTION AND SOUL SEARCH

Ask yourself this question:

Where do I want to steer *my* boat? This is your mission statement for life:

_____

_____

_____

_____

I hope you will feel empowered to make choices that are right for you, even when outside influences cause your sails to billow.

Chapter 3
The Purpose of Money

"After you alchemize your limiting stories, you will see the light instead of the dark."

— Kathryn Eriksen, The Story Alchemist

WHAT ARE YOU DOING WITH your life?

Sometimes I want to scream this question at the top of my lungs. I even scream it at myself from time to time.

I see so many people going through their lives without direction or goals. They are just living from day to day, paycheck to paycheck, and continually saying, "I will start saving tomorrow."

In the meantime, they are not living their lives right now. They are *stressed*. They buy things, hoping those things will fill an unknown void, will bring a happiness they cannot quite grasp. They are not sure where or how to find happiness. Obviously, many of us are searching for joy and happiness, considering the number of spiritual and personal growth books flooding the bookstore shelves.

Yet, here's the thing: To move forward, you must understand that "Happiness does not come from money. Happiness comes from living your life in a way that is purposeful."

I can already hear some of you heckling, "Yeah, but money sure does help a lot!"

Stick with me here.... Wealth is a by-product of purpose and productivity. If you feel you have a career with purpose, you are passionate and engaged in your career. Work is not as much "work" as a "calling." If your personal life outside work is fulfilling, you are excited to go to work, and you are excited to come home. You do not need to "escape" for a vacation. A vacation may be something extra and above.

Imagine for a moment if your vacation could be every day...coming home to a life you love, and loving your work. If it's not, what are your first steps to change?

In her book *Toxic People*, Marsha Petrie Sue offers an ultimatum for people stuck in a negative cycle. I had the opportunity to hear her speak several years ago. She's this petite, blonde fireball with a sweet Southern accent. I could tell she was the kind of lady who could scrap in a bar fight if put to it.

Her ultimatum for dealing with toxic people is simple:

"You can take it, you can change it, or you can leave it. It's just that simple! And if the person stuck refuses to take your advice, YOU leave *them*."

What if the person stuck in a negative cycle is you?

Let's take this a step further. In her book *Mastering Your Mean Girl*, Melissa Ambrosini asks, "What if *you* are your own worst enemy?"

You can't leave yourself, so if you want to get unstuck, you need to learn to love yourself more, talk to yourself positively as you would to a friend, and as Melissa says, "Become your own bestie."

In relation to money, purposeful wealth comes down to creating positive messages about the money we have and looking at how we can improve our satisfaction in our work and play, regardless of the money in our wallets. Winning the lottery might help in the short term, but if you are not ready for it, you will get stuck back in the same patterns, and the money will disappear. According to a 2018 statistic by National Endowment for Financial Education (NEFE), 70 percent of lottery winners go broke within five years of receiving their winnings!

Michael B. Kelley and Pamela Engel did an exposé in *Business Insider* a few years ago about the dark side of lottery winnings. They featured twenty-one horror stories of huge lottery winners who lost it all, some even losing the lives of the loved ones around them, or their own lives. The reality show *The Lottery Changed My Life* frequently features not just the glamour, but the struggle with being thrust into sudden, unexpected monetary wealth.

Here are some questions to consider about money:

REFLECTION AND SOUL SEARCH

1. If you feel you must make more money, what can you do to get on that path?

_____

_____

_____

_____

2. If you get the money you dream of, how will it affect your relationships?

_____

_____

_____

_____

3. How will having more money affect your day-to-day routines?

_____

_____

_____

4. Could you learn to find satisfaction in the income you currently have?

_____

_____

_____

5. What do the above answers reveal to you?

_____

_____

_____

An old Sheryl Crow song, "Soak Up the Sun," gets stuck in my head whenever I hear someone complain about being stuck in a dead-end job. The song describes a woman who is happy regardless of her dead-end job. If we know what we really want—in her case, time to enjoy the sun—every other unimportant thing falls away.

Over my years working with clients, I've discovered two powerful questions that shape one's destiny with money. These two questions determine whether you will spend foolishly or wisely.

With every purchase, every meal, every time you open your wallet filled with credit and debit cards (and hopefully, cash), there are two things to ask yourself:

1. How does this expense impact my life?

2. What is the real purpose I am trying to serve by this expense?

If you ask yourself these two questions daily, not as rhetorical questions, but as a mantra, you will discover your answers. Some days you may be frustrated when you look at yourself in the mirror. Other days you may be filled with gratitude as you tick off the steps you are taking in your life to be your best self, and how you used money the day before, or how you intend to use money today, to achieve your dreams.

Before you move on to the next chapter, where we'll start discussing those dreams, answer those two questions for yourself about something you just purchased or something you are thinking about purchasing in the near future.

REFLECTION AND SOUL SEARCH

1. How does this expense impact my life?

_____

_____

_____

2. What is the real purpose I am trying to serve by this expense?

_____

_____

_____

Chapter 4
Hold Fast to Your Dreams

"Hold fast to dreams, for if dreams die, life is a broken-winged bird that cannot fly."

— Langston Hughes

I MET STEPHANIE FELICIANO SEVERAL YEARS ago at RYLA (Rotary Youth Leadership Awards). RYLA is a leadership camp for high school students. I have helped facilitate this camp in Wisconsin for several years. As a humanitarian, my focus has been to help youth with leadership and volunteerism, and I have met hundreds, if not thousands, of kids, including at RYLA. Stephanie was a student at the camp, and while she was there, she participated in an experience, "The Reality Store." In this exercise, the students choose where they will be at age twenty-five. Stephanie chose that she had two children. As she stepped into the Reality Store, she began to use her money to buy housing, a car, childcare, and health insurance. She spun the Wheel of Fortune, where she had the chance to win a lottery, or get an unexpected bill. Stephanie was blown away by the cost of childcare. She didn't realize how much it would cost for an apartment, houses, cars, and insurance, or how hard it would be to save money.

"I was glad I had the opportunity to play The Reality Store game," Stephanie shared with me. "My eyes were opened, seeing all of those money realities at a young age."

Stephanie had another life-changing experience she shared with me. We've both attended the Hugh O'Brian Youth Leadership Seminar (HOBY), although I attended many years before her. I've found that those who embrace this experience come away forever changed. Stephanie realized:

> Although money seems like something that is important, the most important thing is having those personal relationships and support. It's about the little things. It's about what you can give to others that brings fulfillment. Whether it's your time or your money or your talent, you have something to give.

> I still think about my HOBY experience. It was around dinner time, and we had to choose from a hat and pick a color. Then we had to go to a station. Only four people had a station with a full buffet of food. Another station only had peanut butter and jelly sandwiches and juice. I was only given a scoop of rice, beans, and water. It changed my view of what's important in life. I was so hungry that night. At dinner, a riot started. The facilitators formed a line to keep those who were rioting away from the four people who were eating all this food. I could see how this could happen in real life. How grateful I am to have what I have. I went to bed that night hungry. Although I had cookies in my room, I didn't eat them to remind myself that there are people everywhere who don't have enough to eat. My stomach was growling. Since then, I don't waste as much food. I value what I have. Some people are not that lucky. Not just people in other countries. Right here.

Stephanie, in her short life, is not a stranger to the bumps in the road. Over the years, I forgot about her. Then I saw this post from her on social media:

> To whoever feels like giving up on their dreams...don't throw in the towel.

I remember, four years ago, sitting down with a notebook and planning what my life was supposed to look like by the time I was twenty-two. I was supposed to have been accepted into a top university right after high school. I was supposed to have known (at eighteen years old! Is that even completely realistic?) what I wanted to do for the rest of my life. And I was supposed to have graduated college with honors and applied to dental school.... But life has a funny way of not going as planned.

I was so hard on myself when I didn't see my life going the way I had pictured. I felt like I was disappointing everyone around me. I was so embarrassed that I had failed college classes. I felt like it was too late to reach my goals and a waste of time and money. I felt like I could never live up to the expectations I "thought" people had of me.

But then, in my lowest point, I decided to try something new. I decided to follow my heart and do things that make *me* happy.... In doing that, I discovered I didn't want to become a dentist after all, but instead, I want to be a dental hygienist.

I also discovered another passion while following my heart. Baking! I baked pie crusts until I no longer would burn the bottoms and mixed frostings until I ran out of sugar. I worked countless hours advertising my (now) business, and I continue to push forward into something that made me happy when I was feeling so low.

Not everyone will understand the sacrifice you'll have to make to reach your goals. Some people will call you selfish, might stop talking to you, and might even wait for you to fail.

But let them keep waiting. Do what makes you happy and make a career out of it.

My support system has even dwindled down to a faithful few. And if that happens to you, keep moving forward. As hard as it may be, understand that some people are only meant for a season. Those who are meant to stay with you will understand your sacrifice.

I write this to remind you that you're not alone. Feeling like you've failed is tough. But you have the power to change your perspective. View your failures as lessons and grow from them. Continue chasing those dreams. Make attainable goals, complete them, and always have the big picture in mind. Follow your heart and do what makes you happy. Don't compare your achievements to someone else's. Understand that you're going to make mistakes along the way, and that's okay. Life happens, but don't let that stop you. It's never too late to reach your goals. No more excuses. You can do it.

I'm grateful God's plans were not my plans because here I am at twenty-two years old.... Not where I thought I'd be, but instead, where I'm supposed to be. Following my heart and chasing new dreams.

I knew I needed to interview Stephanie to find out what makes her tick. I wanted to know what prompted her post. I learned a lot from her during our interview, and her words were so powerful that I want to share the full interview here:

What prompted you to post this on social media?

I was having a conversation with a peer. She was struggling with what she wanted to do in her life and wanted to give up. A lot more people are probably in that situation than we realize. It doesn't matter how old you are—be passionate about it; chase after it.

When you fail, how do you pick yourself up?

I was taking up pre-dentistry in college, thinking about being a dentist. Classes were more challenging than I thought. I wanted to take a leap year, but didn't. I failed many of the classes and took it very hard. I thought I wasn't good enough to do what I wanted. Finally, I realized I was trying to do what I thought my parents and others had wanted for me, but I had to think about what I had to do. I took a break from my college courses and looked for volunteer positions at dental offices. A job opened doing sterilization. I saw what it took to be a dentist, and realized I didn't want to be a dentist. I changed how I thought about it, and didn't look at it as a failure, but a shift, a change in how I thought about it, and I've moved on.

How did you do that?

It wasn't easy, but I allowed myself to have an open mind and go into the dental environment to see what it takes. I learned there are different options in the dental field that are more appealing to me. I am my hardest critic. If I am having a hard time living up to my goals, sometimes I feel stuck. I have to challenge myself to see what I learned. That mindset really helped me change the way I approach my goals.

Do you have a tip to change mindset?

It took a long time—three years—for me to have that full mindset shift. I have to remind myself that I am worth it, I can do it, though I may not see that light at the end of the tunnel right now.

It's also really important not to compare myself to others.

Never compare yourself to others. Once I started to look only at myself and my accomplishments, I was able to find a little victory in every single day. Remind yourself that you are worth it, you can do it, and look for little victories in every single day.

Little steps; eventually, you will reach it.

I started my cake business to pay for my education. It started as a hobby and turned into something bigger than I thought it would be. I'm trying to follow my heart. I have gotten a lot more attention because of my baking.

I am also working at a dental office as a dental assistant, trying to make enough money for school. I'm a dental assistant right now but trying to become a dental hygienist. I work there thirty-two hours a week. After work, I go to school two hours, and I'm home by 8 p.m. Then I fill baking orders from 8 to 11 p.m. I wake at 5 a.m. to study. I also record my lectures and listen to them on my commutes. I study at lunch break. Friday is my "day off," and I use that time to promote my baking business on social media. I do deliveries on weekends, and just try to enjoy the rest of my time off.

When I finish school, I'd like to volunteer and do cleanings for free for people who don't have dental care. Right now, I donate cakes and cupcakes through church to kids who can't afford a birthday cake. I also offer cookies and give them away for different events. I feel it's a good way to help out. If you have a skill or talent, it's important to share that skill.

Wow! That seems like a lot. Do you feel like giving up?

About once a week, I feel so tired I have to sit down and force myself to relax. If I don't do that, I start to feel overwhelmed. There's a bigger picture, so I have to keep on pushing forward.

What do you do to relax?

I really like to paint and read. Reading takes me to a place where I don't have to focus. I do my own Do-It-Yourself facials and nails. I like to paint my mom and my sister's nails. Anything that is kind of artsy helps me relax.

What is your history and money story?

My parents were very hardworking and didn't want me to worry about whatever financial situation they were going through. My parents were lower income, living paycheck to paycheck. Their lives have improved a little bit, but it's still a struggle for them.

They have tried to help as best they can, but they didn't have any money saved for me. They took out a loan for my older sister. I was lucky to receive and had to rely on a couple of grants. My parents tried their best to help me, but the money was always an issue, though they would never admit it. My dad has worked overtime and does side jobs to provide anything I need when I've come short on my tuition. It's not that they haven't wanted to help, and they've always tried to fill in the gaps.

I don't like the idea of debt. I even regret paying for a car off the lot and wish I had bought an old beater because I'm still paying off the car. I don't like to worry constantly about paying bills. I would rather save up and pay for something when I have the money to do so. I don't like to stress anyone else out about my money, like my parents.

Sometimes I have to sacrifice. I could have finished school earlier with loans or finished later without loans. Not having anything to worry about at the end of it is what was most important to me.

Sometimes shadows from your past can haunt you, like the "Ghost of Christmas Past." What shadow have you dealt with regarding money?

The shadow comes with seeing the struggle other people go through with money. It's such a burden to have to live paycheck to paycheck, and it's something I don't want to do. I don't want to have to worry where the money is coming from next to pay a light bill or my car bill. I see so many people struggling, and I don't want to bring my future family into something where I'm in debt and can't go on vacation because I have to pay bills. I also don't want my future partner to have to come into that in my life.

What is your favorite quote?

"Live like no one else so you can live like no one else" from Dave Ramsey.

What was your turning point in your relationship with money?

Three moments happened. I didn't save anything, was getting paid bi-weekly. This was about two years ago when I was working as a dental assistant. I had gotten a little raise and I thought money grew on trees.

When I went to the store, my debit card got declined. I couldn't understand why it got declined. My bank had stopped my purchases. I had $50 in my account. My mindset was ridiculous. I thought, "I have money and can do whatever I want." What I was purchasing was not even necessities—more stuff I wanted, not needed.

It was so embarrassing, so I never want that to happen again.

The following week, I had wisdom teeth extracted and couldn't afford the bill. I had to ask my parents to help.

Then, I couldn't afford the next semester of college because it became more expensive than I had thought.

What was your epiphany?

I realized the importance of not just spending, but also saving for emergencies. First thing first...I need to save money. Second, I don't want to live a life where I need to worry about money. When you have that worry about money, it takes away your joy, your peace, and it makes you an angrier person.

I wasn't myself when I was worried about payments. I didn't want to live like this.

How did you change it?

I spoke to my cousin, who gave me a couple of tips. Every paycheck, I took out 10-15 percent and put it in a savings account. I had to budget and plan how much everything would cost. I took out an allowance of $20-25 a week. I'm not a person who usually goes out to coffee shops, but it was my fun money. I had to keep in mind it was only $20-25 a week. If I didn't spend it, it went to savings. I had this allowance for myself, and I learned that I had to be strict with what I was doing. What really helped me is that a little less than two years ago, I started putting sticky notes everywhere. Every day, I was reading the sticky notes, and it started to change the way I saw my finances.

It was extremely uncomfortable at first. I was used to spending my money however I wanted. The moment I decided things had to change [the most]...was in my car. I started putting little Post-it notes on the visor to remind myself. I bought granola snacks and kept non-perishable food in my glove compartment to keep me from going through the drive-thru. I stayed a step ahead and kept whatever I needed in my car, so I didn't impulse buy. I also brought fruit and other healthy snacks for at work.

I don't have as many sticky notes anymore. Eight months ago, I took them off.... I used to have at least ten notes on my visor. I even had one telling me, "Don't go through Chic-fil-A today."

What were some of your other notes?

"You can do it!"

By the change cup in my car, I had, "Think twice; do you really need that?"

"Is this a need, or is this a want? If it's a want, can I save up for it?"

"Is this an impulse buy?"

"Don't give up."

"Focus on the big picture."

"It's easy to swipe my card, but it's not easy to make the next payment."

I'm down to one message in my car: "Focus on the big picture."

How have the messages you tell yourself about money improved?

My perspective on money has changed. Money still has a lot of value, but it doesn't have as much power over me as it once did. It's not a constant struggle. I'm able to live a better life and be at peace because I have money saved up to do what I need, and also what I want.

Although it's not at a point where I can help as many people as I would like, I don't have to worry as much, and it's a great feeling.

Why is it important to help others?

So many people are struggling, and I know how good it feels to relax for a day. Some people can't take that opportunity to ease their minds and can't provide for their families. If you can help somebody else, do it. I feel that it always will come back around. I may not have seen that help financially personally, but I've had things where someone's helped me change a flat tire, so I think it all comes back to you. It brings so much joy to me, and to those people I'm helping. We shouldn't rely on other people to help; we need to take accountability for ourselves, but if you have the opportunity to help others, take it. If you have relationships and support, it will be there when you need it, too.

I hope you enjoyed Stephanie's interview and found it helpful. To me, her advice about sticky notes was particularly useful. Remember what she said? "What really helped me is that a little less than two years ago, I started putting sticky notes everywhere. Every day I was reading the sticky notes, it started to change the way I saw my finances."

You can create sticky notes and affirmations for your love life or any other area of your life, as well as for your finances. Moving yourself from a financial or emotional hole always goes back to your mindset. If you dwell in a land of darkness, you will stay stuck in that barren plain.

Take some time now to reflect on what you learned in this chapter and apply it to your life.

REFLECTION AND SOUL SEARCH

In the spaces below, I invite you to think about habits you have that you need to change and what kinds of sticky notes you can write for yourself to help accomplish that change.

Today's Date:
Bad Habit #1:

Sticky Note #1:

Location that will help me change this habit. I am going to put this sticky note here:

Date I will check back to see how this behavior changed:

Reflection on date I check back:

Today's Date:
Bad Habit #2:

Sticky Note #2:

Location that will help me change this habit. I am going to put this sticky note here:

Date I will check back to see how this behavior changed:

Reflection on date I check back:

Today's Date:
Bad Habit #3:

Sticky Note #3:

Location that will help me change this habit. I am going to put this sticky note here:

Date I will check back to see how this behavior changed:

Reflection on date I check back:

FOCUS ON THE BIG PICTURE...
What are you doing with your life?

I told Stephanie she was wise beyond her years. I wish I had been that smart when I was her age.

It took me a little bit longer than Stephanie, but I no longer think about money in terms of scarcity, or even abundance. I think of my life, my money, and my time in terms of *purpose.*

What Is the Purpose?

The answer to my own sticky note, "What am I doing with my life? What is the real purpose that I am trying to serve?" is *the* wakeup call. It is the call to *presence.* Personally, my answer is "*Today,* I will live my best day." I actually followed Stephanie's lead and put a note,

"Today I will live my best day. I am loved and grateful," on the mirror in my bathroom so it is the first thing I see when I wake up.

The note that inspires you will probably be a different note than what inspires Stephanie, or what inspires me.

In Chapter 12: Flip the Script, we will have an exercise to help you home in on the best, most positive Money Messages to inspire you. Knowing which Money Messages and life messages inspire you will make the difference between using your money for a purpose and frivolously or carelessly spending it until it's completely gone.

Having a proper money and lifestyle mindset will make the difference between embracing the day or going back to bed to catch another thirty minutes of sleep. (That doesn't really help you, by the way.) It's a mental "shift," as Wayne Dyer calls it.

> Toward the end of Wayne Dyer's life, he made a movie titled *The Shift*. It was filmed at the Asilomar retreat center in California. The movie explores the choices several unconnected couples make, couples at different stages in their lives, and how they find ways to come back to center. Though it's not stated directly in the movie, Wayne Dyer was battling leukemia at the time. Throughout the movie, it's as though Wayne Dyer was the angel, watching, counseling, and guiding people to reflect on what is important in life.

My son and I pilgrimaged to Asilomar on the coast of Northern California a few years after Wayne Dyer passed away. My son, only nine at the time, had no clue about Wayne Dyer, the retreat center, or what this trip meant to me. My own finances had stabilized since my divorce and I'd made a huge shift in my career, so this trip with him was my reward. Because my heart was still exceedingly sad, this trip was my effort to connect with and reflect upon the peace and calm that was Wayne Dyer at the end of his life.

Reflective, peaceful, and calm are not words normally associated with a nine-year-old boy, and my son did not disappoint. He tore down the beach path like a little Tasmanian devil. Tearing off his shoes, a spray of sand followed as he raced from the beach to the ocean. My little boy was thrilled to have a chance to run around the edge of the ocean waves, getting his pants and feet wet and sandy. He made mud snowballs and giggled with the abandon of a child who has not yet felt the weight of the world. I still felt a lot of weight on my shoulders; I was still worried about whether I could make it on this massive blue planet and be a positive role model to my child after the cataclysmic "shift" called "divorce." At first, I needed to force myself to move forward and get my feet in the sand and surf. Seeing my son being such a goof, I couldn't help but laugh and forget my worries for a moment. As we played and laughed on the beach, I felt more and more like the child I remembered from the plains of North Dakota, with muddy hands and wind-blown hair. We threw mud snowballs into the waves.

It was warm for the season, but there was still a chill by the ocean that November day. The cold felt tingly on my skin, and a sense of peace washed over me. *"We are going to be okay, no matter what,"* I whispered to myself with a contented smile. I shivered with the realization of my mind shift. Being there, in the salty breeze, feeling the spray of the ocean, and sharing those moments with my son—those are still some of my favorite memories. We preserved them in pictures, taking selfies by the ocean. One of those pictures is preserved on the back cover of this book. After the beach, my son had fun clowning around on the twin grand cypress trees that framed the trail to the beach, like a giant gateway from here...to there.

REFLECTION AND SOUL SEARCH

Where is your "here"—the place you are presently that you maybe don't want to be?

_____

_____

_____

Where is your "there"—the place you would like to be in the future?

_____

_____

_____

The next chapter will delve into the choices we make about money, and how to move past some of the blocks we face in getting from "here" to "there."

*I*F YOU HAVE CHILDREN, YOU may also want to create a healthy environment around Money Messages for your children. I want my son to have every advantage of my savings as he begins his adult life, but I also want him to build his own future. Warren Buffett once said, "You should leave your children enough so they can do anything, but not enough so they can do nothing."

Chapter 5
Conscious Money Choices

"Know what you own, and know why you own it."

— Peter Lynch

*W*HAT IS THE PURPOSE OF your money?

Asking this question initiates the practice of making conscious money choices.

That purpose we are trying to serve could be fun, if the money is available. I'm not saying you can't enjoy your money. I earmark a certain amount of money each month for pure fun. I also try not to get too wrapped up in the details. Instead of agonizing over a purchase that seems frivolous, I know how much I can spend in a month for fun, and after that point, I'm just done! Knowing exactly *how* you can purpose your money is one of the first building blocks for Purposeful Wealth.

Writing this book was a huge next step for me in helping more people to hear my words my way. Being introverted, I just don't do well "on the circuit." I freeze (at least inside) when I must speak in front of a crowd. I would describe myself as an "extroverted introvert." When I am passionate enough to speak within or to a crowd, I can do it, but it's not a passion of mine, at least not at this point in my life.

Sometimes I get a bit flustered and my words don't come out just right. Speaking publicly to large groups often leaves me exhausted. I'm useless for a day after...total zombie-land. So, I prefer writing to help me communicate exactly what I wish to say.

It's fun for me to share the lessons and passion I have for conscious spending and using money with a purpose. It's not terrifying or exhausting for me to write, and it gives me the opportunity to help people escape being dragged down an emotional rabbit hole when thinking about money.

The choice to write this book, however, was not without expense. When Karen Putz reached out to me, after I put out the call for a writing coach and/or co-author, I had to pay her money for her services. What? A woman who knows her worth and asks for payment for her expertise? I thought it was fantastic, not only that she was very straightforward with her pricing, but that she knew what she wanted to work on and what she didn't want to work on.

I had a dilemma: I had another expense, a business trip, about the same time I wanted to work on this book.

I made a choice to be more careful about my other business expenses for a few months and adjust my spending. Putting money toward something like these two larger, purposeful purchases meant I would need to cut back on purchases and expenses that didn't serve those purposes, at least for a while.

Facebook ads—um, not for at least three months.

Paying for sponsorships, meals with clients, and networking contacts? How about I defer to the next event, or maybe meet at a coffee shop and order tea (having consumed a delicious meal at home before arriving).

I canceled my satellite radio for a while. I stayed in for movies versus going out. Popcorn on the stove is healthier and cheaper (and yummier) than the theatre and microwave popcorn.

These may seem small—sometimes there are bigger sacrifices—but in the name of balance, I prioritized what was most important for my wealth, health, and happiness.

More recently, I bought a new car with more leg room for my very tall family. It felt so good to know I had saved enough to pay for a chunk of the car from savings, considerably lowering my monthly payment. I'm still a work in progress, so my hope for my next car is to write a check for the whole thing and drive it off the lot fully paid. These days, I refuse to go into debt without a realistic plan to come back to the center and be debt-free.

I'm happy to adjust my lifestyle from time to time because I'm using my money purposefully. And I don't have to make sacrifices as much as I used to. I have emergency funds, and I budget accordingly. Now, it's no longer survival or drowning in debt, but temporary comfort versus discomfort. I may choose to make a trade-off for something that serves an important purpose, versus a want or wish that is not as important.

When you are in a place of purposeful spending, you will feel good and excited about your money's purpose.

You are reading this book because something brought you here. I'm guessing you want to feel better about the role of money in your life. I'm guessing you want to figure out how to be healthier, wealthier, and happier.

If you are facing a mountain of debt, a mountain of anxiety about money—there are ways you can experience money in a different way.

If you've done a good job saving, but you are not sure if you are doing the right thing as far as where you put the money, you may ask yourself, "Is there something I could be doing better? Am I missing anything?"

I can help you with that. You can navigate your money journey using the different tools in this book that allow you to "feel" money differently. When we lack money, we may feel paralyzed where we are. But with new knowledge, new tools, and new guides—we can create a whole new journey.

Changing your mindset is not an overnight fix. It takes time and effort. Social media guru Tai Lopez says, "The thing about positive thinking is it takes a while to kick in. It's kind of like lifting weights. You have to keep doing it even when you don't see instant results."

Winners Keep Track

"Winners make a habit of manufacturing their own positive expectations in advance of the event," writes Brian Tracy, self-development author and motivational speaker.

Keeping this wonderful quote in mind, let's be conscious of our progress. I want you to start tracking today.

In terms of your finances, invest in yourself and get some software to track your spending and saving. I don't care what you use. Many great, both simple and complicated, personal and business spending tracking software programs are out there. Pick the one that works for you.

The simplest and handiest, which I personally recommend, is Mint.com. For daily use, I like the mobile app better than the website. At a glance, I can see all my debit, credit, and investment accounts. It doesn't give me an in-depth analysis, but it provides an overview, and I get email reminders on how much I'm spending, and what I'm spending it on. I even set up a budget with it; that part is easier to use on the website than the mobile version. You don't have to work that far ahead, though. For now, let's take it in baby steps.

Awareness helps you to understand your mindset about money. Record your thoughts as you spend money throughout the day. Recognize and acknowledge frustration, negative influences, and feelings of giving up. Also note the moments of joy or gratitude.

Since I have my phone with me all the time, I tend to use its "Notes" app when I'm having a thought. If I'm feeling down or questioning something in my life or my business, I might go on a writing tirade (or voice to text in Notes) about what is itching my brain. Then, when I'm feeling better an hour or a day later, I review those notes and write myself a note about how to look at the situation more objectively next time.

Whether you use sticky notes, a writing journal, a spreadsheet, or an app, keep track of your thoughts *and* your money.

We will revisit your Money Messages throughout this book, but the first step is to begin the mindfulness practice of recognizing your thoughts. Continue to ask yourself: *"What is the real purpose I am trying to serve?"*

Understand the *purpose* of your spending. Be aware of what you are spending. As your mindset changes, I bet you will organically start to see changes in the nastygrams you get from Mint.com. You will be able to take the many, many reminder sticky notes off your visor. You will eventually be free!

REFLECTION AND SOUL SEARCH

Investigate various programs or apps that will help you track your spending and create a budget.

Chapter 6
Money Stories

"Trauma is the string which binds us all together. There are a whole bunch of people out there hurting, that need a safe place to tell their story."

— Theo Fleury, Olympic Superstar and NHL All-Star

EVERYONE HAS A STORY. THE Money Messages we learn, live with, internalize, or overcome all knit together into a history, or a story of our emotional ups and downs. We create an intimate relationship from these experiences with our money.

I find it fascinating that when I mention writing this book to people, many immediately delve into a very deep story about their parents', their loved ones', or their own personal struggles and successes with money. A palpable energy enters the conversation.

Sometimes this energy is wrapped in frustration and anger, but sometimes there is a sense of pride in what people have achieved. Always, there has been a battle won or lost, and the emotions run deep.

Remember, this relationship you have created with money is a story you have created in your mind. The reality of what has happened with your money may be different from the story you tell yourself.

I have met enormously wealthy people who feel a sense of lack. I have met other people with smaller means, who are extremely happy and rich in their mindsets.

A good financial advisor can help you keep a check on those stories and reframe them. Keep in mind that we financial advisors aren't professional therapists. (I do keep a list of great therapists in my arsenal of resources for those situations.) But a trained and seasoned financial professional can help you keep on track—and identify when the emotional side of your money story is being clouded by your biases.

Looking into Your Past

Grownups don't tell us, when we're kids, how to have a positive or negative view of money. Often, parents and teachers never talk to young people about money—at all. But as children, we all absorb clues about money through adults' attitudes and their actions.

An interesting elderly gentleman in my Rotary Club, Richard, was the paper boy for Paul Harris, the founder of Rotary in 1904. Richard has some pretty crazy stories, and at a recent meeting he was in a talkative mood, telling me how he, as a kid, didn't realize Paul Harris was ill and dying. One day, Paul Harris was just gone, and no one would explain "why." Richard said it made an impression on him because back in the day, paper boys had to go door to door to collect their subscription money, and Paul Harris always paid on time and tipped him well. He said children in the 1940s were scooted out the room when adults were talking. Children in his community also didn't attend funerals, and they didn't really understand about rich or poor, and how to handle money, unless their parents taught them.

As a child in the 1970s and '80s, I experienced that adults in my conservative Bible community didn't really talk about money either. I was warned by my elders, "Don't get into deep discussions about money, religion, or sex." I did take Home Ec, or Consumer

Sciences, as they call it these days. I don't think I learned nearly enough to be prepared for adulting, but I did learn about the birds and the bees in a very medical sense, and how to mend a torn shirt, sew a pair of beach shorts, balance a checkbook, create a budget, make a decent Thanksgiving gravy, and determine the cost of a grocery list. There were boys in my Home Ec class, too, so don't think it was a sexist thing. I probably had one of the most feminist Home Ec teachers ever. Her life goal was to empower us to be great adults. Students responded, and her class was one of the most popular in high school.

I think kids today are much more exposed to the realities of adulting, money, and many other subjects. People born after 2000 came of age with debit cards, credit cards, and the exchange of money through apps like Venmo or Zelle—and they are less likely to see or use cash the way earlier generations did. Their concept of money is electronic. The traditional nuclear family has also been blown apart, so there are many varieties and flavors of families. I do believe there's a simple reason for this: The technology age has digitized everything (including the way this book has been authored and revised), and massive amounts of information are now available through the internet. It's much more comprehensible to us that there's more than one way to "do life." We don't have to follow the generations of ancestors before us. Just because Dad was a bricklayer doesn't mean we have to be a bricklayer.

When I was a kid, we were not rich, but we somehow got by, even through the loss of my father's business, and high interest rates in the late 1970s and early '80s that nearly buried my parents. In my naïveté, I never really thought of us as financially struggling. I do, however, vividly remember my cousin, ten years my senior, teasing me that if we had more than four generic products in our house, we were Communists.

I had no idea what a Communist was, but I understood it was "bad." After he left, I started counting: one…two…twenty generic products in our house!

Later, I approached my mother, extremely distressed, "Are the police going to come and take us away because we are Communists?"

My mom obviously thought her imaginative daughter was just being weird again. "What are you talking about? Where did you learn this?"

Mom laughed hard when I explained what my cousin had told me. "No, we're just careful how we spend our money, and generic products help us save money."

Like osmosis, we absorb messages, even if we don't truly understand in the moment what they mean. As you know, I call those "Money Messages." They can be messages interpreted in different ways. How we interpret those messages is intensely personal and unique to each person. You and your siblings may receive the same Money Messages while growing up, but each of you may interpret them in different ways.

If, as a child, you believe the myth that being cost conscious is "bad" or "miserly," how will that affect the way you spend now and into the future?

If you witness a parent spending money and hiding it from their partner, what effect will that have on you when faced with a major purchase?

Ask for Help

I'm going to share the story of a close friend I'll name Stacey who needed help in reinterpreting her Money Messages and wanted advice about her debt situation.

Stacey's mother was a single parent who worked extremely hard to give Stacey and her brother anything they wanted.

Her mother was very knowledgeable about money, balanced a checkbook consistently, and paid every bill on time. What she didn't do well was long-term saving. Whenever the kids wanted something, they got it even if it meant paying with a credit card. Though Stacey's mom kept up with paying off the credit card bills, she would spend instead of saving.

When Stacey was in second grade, her mother remarried. Despite the additional income and adult in the house, Stacey's mom was still the main one holding the family together, especially since Stacey's stepdad's income was unsteady. Having grown up in a family of seven, Stacey's mother didn't want to let her family down, or have her children want for anything as she had done at times growing up. Stacey's mom's need to protect and nurture her family had at times left her overwhelmed and afraid to ask for support.

Stacey's family never clued Stacey or her brother in on where they stood financially or how they were doing with money. Often, her mother would say things like, "It's just money. If you want it, we will get it." Stacey's parents never discussed the value or cost of items. They just took care of the kids.

As Stacey grew and became independent, she discovered the lure of credit. When she "needed" something, she just charged it to her card. She believed the money would just appear, and the credit card would be paid off. Sometimes this worked for her.

Later, as Stacey built her own business, she would think about what she needed for her business, without having the money in hand. She would anticipate new business coming in the door, and she simply believed what she needed would be met with future wealth.

Stacey would feel guilty and buy things for her children. She would donate money she really couldn't afford to her church—even when she was panicking inside that she couldn't even pay her own mortgage that month.

Stacey's husband is a man of modest means. He has a steady job, where he is dedicated to working with children. He allowed Stacey to take full rein of their finances since he didn't feel like he was a "money person." She felt responsible for meeting her family's emotional and physical needs, much as her mother did, and not burdening them with the cost. Her Money Message was, "If you need something, we will get it."

Over a period of years, Stacey's family's debt compounded into the tens of thousands of dollars. As Stacey lay awake late at night, her stress compounded as well.

She was ashamed.

Stacey did not want her husband to know what a mess they were in. Meanwhile, her kids' financial demands only increased as they became involved in extracurricular activities. When the financial burden finally became too much, Stacey approached me for guidance.

We talked about her past and the shame she felt. We talked about the stress that was now affecting her business.

We discovered she was extremely lucky because she had access to what I refer to as a "soft reset button." Stacey had money saved, but she was unsure whether she should save it and struggle on or use it to pay off most of the debt. Stacey was paying upwards of 20 percent interest on her debt, so it didn't make sense to hold on to the money when the markets could only return 4 to 8 percent annually over a ten-year period, depending on the investment.

We started the discussion by talking about how to break the cycle. If Stacey used that soft reset button, it was a one-time shot. How would she prevent herself and her family from getting right back into the same situation five years from now?

I gave suggestions, but mainly, I let Stacey take ownership. My first suggestion was to use some of the money as an active emergency fund (which I will refer to later as a "bucket," something you fill up), to create an environment and feeling of living with cash instead of credit. We brought her husband into the conversation. Stacey needed support, and she found that her husband was not only compassionate, but eager to help. He had observed her progression into despair, but he was afraid to ask what the problem was. He didn't want to put extra pressure on her by bugging her about finances.

First, they looked at the reality of living in debt. They looked at her husband's income; it was consistent, but not enough to pay for their entire lifestyle. Stacey's income could sometimes be large, but it was sporadic. They looked in-depth at their budget, and how they might live mostly on just his income. The second step was to figure out how to use her income more effectively.

Their finances were very confusing because they had multiple business and personal credit cards. We simplified it down to one card for business, and one card for personal, and those cards stayed at home in a drawer. If they wanted to make a purchase on credit, this method gave them time to go home and think about it—preventing impulse purchases. The goal was to consolidate some of the debt and improve their credit rating. Some people may be tempted to cut up or close all their cards. I don't advise either method. If you just cut up all the cards, the revolving credit limit is still there, and the accounts are still open. Having several forgotten lines of credit makes you more susceptible to identity theft. A nice clean credit report is easier to review and monitor. However, closing *all* your cards is not the answer, either. It is good to have some credit lines open to show you can use revolving credit responsibly.

Stacey and her husband switched to operating on a cash basis. They used the soft reset button to pay off most of the other cards. The money no longer going toward those card payments was now used to create an emergency fund. They also paid more than the monthly minimum on the smaller, more manageable debt. We worked out a plan to enable them to be debt free in less than five years, while still working on a cash basis and saving in tandem. They have continued to work to save six months of living expenses for their emergency fund.

Any new money Stacey gained from her business was no longer spent as it was earned or spent based on potential business in the pipeline. A portion of it went into the emergency savings bucket. A portion was earmarked to pay quarterly taxes for her business. A portion was going toward the family budget, in a savings account, to refill the bucket for their family, to meet future shortfalls due to a dry spell in her business, and to meet the small shortfall from her husband's income. A portion was going into a special savings account just for her business and future business development expenses. And a portion was going to replenish the money used for the soft reset button.

All that restructuring occurred about six months ago. When I recently checked in with Stacey, her business was flourishing. She hadn't realized how much the stress about money was affecting her ability to focus on her business. Stacey is now making more money than ever before, and she and her husband have made good progress on the emergency fund. They haven't increased their debt, and although they haven't paid down as much as they planned, the remaining debt is getting whittled away.

Stacey also realized how much of an effect the compounding interest of her credit cards was impeding her ability to get ahead. She told me it's easier to save money now—and they are always looking at ways they can still enjoy life and save money at the same time.

"Healing takes time, and asking for help is a courageous step."

— Mariska Hargitay,
Star of *Law & Order: SVU*

Often, we use impulse purchases to fill a void created by exhaustion and stress. Instead of letting stress lead the family to fast food restaurants, Stacey now plans meals on Sundays and incorporates the food preparation into family time as a bonding activity, as opposed to letting her family watch TV or do other activities while she takes full responsibility for their meals. Her kids might be chopping vegetables while she is washing salad. They visit about their week, as they work together as a family. She has not only engaged her husband, but also her children, in being successful at the family finances. Her oldest son works and is saving for college. He's also being cost conscious of the universities he's visiting, and he's keeping his earnings potential in balance with how much he wishes to take out in student loans.

Stacey and her family store meals for the week that are easy to prepare when things are hectic or her energy level is low; meals that are pre-prepped and easy to freeze, assemble, or reheat are packaged in her freezer in just the right portions for each meal. How many people these days order boxed meal pre-prep kits and pay four times the food cost just for the convenience of pre-prepped healthy food? You still must cook it! And really, pre-preparing meals for an entire week only takes an hour or two on Sunday.

Stacey also looks at how she can make multiple meals from one ingredient. I shared this little tip with her when she was despairing about how to feed her family with growing boys. She joked with me that I should write a recipe book on how to feed a family with less money after I finish this one. (We'll see. Check out my money-saving food prep tips in the Bonus Section.)

As Stacey and I sat together, I could see a different person. This woman was in charge and loving life. Though she is still super-busy, I didn't detect the stress I had felt six months earlier. She surprised me. She said they had just recently downgraded their cable package, realizing they mostly rented movies anyway. They went to an online streaming movie service using their smart TV. Stacey decided the extra savings would go toward her retirement fund. She really wants to get ahead, not just catch up, and she feels she is ready to do it. Now, when she feels like she needs something, she looks at what is available and makes the most with what they have. She has been creative in using interns and job bartering to get things done that she used to pay more to outsource.

Stacey said when she first started making changes, she was in a panic. She felt like she was giving up something. But with my encouragement, and the support of her husband and kids, she started to see she was living a life of greater abundance and connection with her family than when she was waiting for abundance to come to her.

Chapter 7
Turning Points:
My Money Story

"Remember that just because you hit bottom doesn't mean you have to stay there."

— Robert Downey, Jr.

*T*HINK BACK ON YOUR LIFE· When have you hit rock bottom and had a turning point? Think about this: You are always one decision away from having a turning point in your life.

AdaPia d'Errico, who has been featured on TED Talks and Goalcast, has a poignant story of transformation. She blew up the "picture perfect life" to live her most authentic life. She went from being an Italian housewife to a real estate investor, yoga expert, and corporate leadership facilitator. "I had all these stories of what I thought other people wanted," she says. For nine years, she lived a lie, in a childless marriage, delaying having children, though her husband wished for a family. On the surface, it was the picture-perfect story of love and marriage, but when she went to visit a friend who had a baby, she realized being a mom was not the life that would make her happy. She took a risk to be something other than what she thought society told her to be. For many women, leaving the confines of "a happy traditional marriage" is still unacceptable at best, scandalous at worst. But her lifestyle, the happy traditional marriage, was a façade that was killing her heart. She couldn't continue living a lie. She created a new story, more authentic to her soul. She wanted to be free, be financially independent, and have her own voice. She left everything. Then, she called her father for support, which was extremely difficult for her. She was so afraid to disappoint him. He told her to come home, and she rebuilt a new life, the life she, not anyone else, dreamed for herself. Through her eclectic experience, and transforming her story for herself, AdaPia healed. If you would like to hear her full TED Talk, I've included it in the "TED Talk" Bonus Section.

> *"As I create meaningful change in myself, I am able to help others through sharing my process, my reflections and my stories. My story healed me. Our stories heal us. We can all learn from our own, and each other's experiences."*
>
> — AdaPia d'Errico

I'm about to share some very personal stuff now about my own life and money story, and my vulnerabilities. I almost didn't put this in the book because it's still a source of shame for me many years later. But Karen Putz, who helped me every step of the way in making this book a reality, gave me encouragement. I reached out, and I'm glad I did. Karen told me, "I really like how you opened up here. There are several lessons entwined: taking back your power, recognizing your strengths, flipping your Money Messages, and asking for help when needed."

So here goes…

During and after college, I bootstrapped and eked out a living by "working hard." This was my initial, inherited Money Message from my community and environment growing up: Work hard. Make enough money to survive. Die.

Deep down, I felt we all have a higher purpose in this world than the pursuit of money. This belief, about having purpose and pursuing our passions for the greater good, still rings true to me. Today, however, I don't believe money is bad. I have evolved to believe money is useful. It is not necessary, nor is it healthy, to ignore our personal health and happiness. We also need to be aware of our financial health, but not to let it dominate our lives.

Let's look at my first real job, my first experience with sacrifice and power, and then I'll return to more positive messages about purpose and wealth.

Here I was, in the mid-1990s, a junior high and high school teacher in my first job. I was thrilled to have any job, after substitute teaching and working several side jobs for over a year after college. The teaching market was competitive because the two colleges on that side of North Dakota specialized in transforming women into teachers and housewives.

Most career-driven teachers left the state for better opportunities. But my boyfriend had a good job, so it would have meant leaving him. A woman's value and monetary net worth were still strongly determined by the value of the man she was with. Women were usually paid less than men, and surviving solo was difficult. It would have meant giving up my value as a woman. Starting over? Not even a consideration then.

The job was at a small rural school. I knew deep down it was not a "good" job. It was low paying with a lot of responsibility. I taught junior high English, led the drama club, assisted the speech coach, supervised the honor society, and served as a school and public librarian to boot. In my spare time, I was required to chaperone other school activities like football games. I worked over seventy hours a week. I had no dedicated prep periods during school because I had to staff the public and school library by myself when not in class.

In this small town, I first discovered library patrons who became obsessed with series book authors like Anne Rice, Nora Roberts, Tom Clancy, and J. K. Rowling. They would excitedly chat with me about the plot of the latest novel they were reading. The elderly ladies and men were a pleasure. I loved my kids and the parents, especially the ones excited about education and reading. I felt a sense of accomplishment when I helped a migrant worker's son start reading books and discuss them with excitement during our tutoring sessions. He advanced his reading aptitude nearly a full grade level in less than five months. Unfortunately, a month later, he disappeared, without explanation. When I asked the school secretary, she flippantly replied, "Oh, many of the migrant workers head to other states after the harvest. He might be back next year."

The school was a dichotomy of wealth and poverty. On one side were very wealthy families, the management and corporate farmers who directed the operations of the sugar factory and supplied its input: sugar beets. The processing smelled putrid. My boyfriend and I joked that it smelled like a "poopy diaper factory." The principal at the school said that was "the smell of money."

On the other side were poor white factory workers and migrant Mexican farm workers. Their children, who didn't dress as nicely, often looked tired, and sometimes were hungry. You could instantly tell which side of the fence kids were from by how they dressed, spoke, and behaved.

I was constantly butting heads with the superintendent and principal, requesting funds to buy books that library patrons desperately wanted to read. I wanted to get library books in Spanish, and textbooks that focused on English as a second language, and I wanted to restructure classes to foster students from the top to the bottom, at the reading level they were at upon walking in to my class. We had some seventh graders reading at a ninth-grade level, and others at a second-grade level. It was frustrating and nearly impossible to engage all students at the same time, in the same class, with the textbooks I was given. For those who loved reading, the public library was a haven. It was the mid-1990s, so the internet was still not commonplace. The library or video store was still the way people escaped into a world of fantasy and excitement.

My dream had been to pursue my life's passion as a teacher, and I still cherish those moments. I wish I could have used my French teaching degree, too, but there was no opportunity. On a limited budget, in a community that poured more money into the administrators' salaries and football than anything else, I was lucky to put on a school play with a small budget. I wanted to shake up the status quo and teach kids about critical thinking, plus share some of the magic I had discovered traveling to Europe and going to college for a year in France. I did not come from money, but I had not let that stop me. I got scholarships, worked hard, and used sheer determination to make my education unforgettable and to travel. I was young, naive, hopeful, idealistic, and a bit stubborn.

I was dismayed with the school administration—in particular, the principal, who intimidated and harassed me. He would never get away with what he did in today's #metoo generation. I was contractually required to live in the town; my salary of $17,000 a year equated to a tiny, dingy, one-bedroom apartment. My home and my boyfriend were in another town forty-five minutes away. Plus, I had more than $45,000 (about $75,000 in today's dollars) in school loans and student-teaching survival debt.

In my little shanty apartment, I kept my windows and curtains tightly shut. I put a rolled-up towel on the floor in front of my front door so the smell of my cigarettes wouldn't drift into the hallway. I chain-smoked, drank coffee, and graded papers late into the night, preparing lesson plans for the first time. My eyes burned with tears of frustration and exhaustion in the haze of smoke due to the room's poor air circulation.

High school boys, and sometimes parents, drove by to see if they could spy on what the new, young, single-lady teacher was doing. I would peek out from time to time, and sometimes catch cars parked, idling one story below, kids peering out of the car windows. Occasionally, I would find beer bottles on the lawn below my window.

One day, after my boyfriend had visited me, the principal called me into his office.

"You know," he said, "our community has standards, especially for our young women."

My face flushed hot.

Silence.

"I'm not sure what you're talking about," I stammered.

"Listen, girl; if you want to sleep with men as a single teacher, you need to do it elsewhere. It was brought to my attention you had a boy at your apartment."

I fought back tears. Instead of fighting back, instead of telling him it was none of his business what I did in my private residence, I felt small. "I'm so sorry," I said. "It's my boyfriend. He just came up to visit because I had so much work. I didn't have time to drive home. He just came up, we ate spaghetti, and I graded papers."

"Did he sleep there overnight?"

"Er, um, yes. He left early this morning."

He slammed his hand on his desk. "That is unacceptable. We are a Christian community with hometown values. If I ever hear that he stays overnight here again before you are married, you won't have a job. Am I clear?"

Everything blurred, tears streamed, and I couldn't talk. My face was on fire, and hotter tears started to burn my cheeks. The only thing clear was the sneer on his face as he leaned back, legs spread-eagled, exposing his fat belly. I was frozen for what seemed like an eternity. I'm not even sure what I said, if I said anything. My ears rang. I turned and ran to my library office, sobbing. But I didn't have time to think. My class started in ten minutes. I had to go and pull myself together.

I was called into the principal's office another time because he was concerned about the school and my reputation when another single-lady teacher and I went for a beer at the local bar. The other teacher had convinced me we needed to get out more. It wasn't like I had danced on the tables and sung drunken carols to a saloon piano player. It was simply a quiet night, a beer, and some friendly bonding while a jukebox played country songs in the background. A couple of older, married teachers came by and said hello.

The other single teacher also got called into the office, like a puppy that had just piddled. She never asked me to go out for a beer again, but she did tell me what a misogynist the principal was.

Being a person of deep, spiritual faith, but also a suppressed bohemian, I was confused and humiliated by these interactions, but also defiant.

I made the decision to go home each weekend, regardless of the weather, and I refused to chaperone any more weekend events, despite the principal's petulant yelling.

The harassment continued. He refused to let me take parent chaperones on a trip for a student organization I supervised, saying it was too expensive to pay for extra adults. He even refused to let me have chaperones after a parent offered to pay for their own room.

So, even though I was fearful, I took the students on a trip by myself in the school van. Of course, like Murphy's Law, we got snowed in the last day of the conference. The principal thought I should brave the dangerous four-hour journey back with the students as scheduled. It was a zero-visibility blizzard in North Dakota with very slippery road conditions. You just don't mess with Mother Nature. I grappled with the decision.

The conference was over. It was nearly 11 a.m. and close to check-out time. I was stressed. Many of the schools were having their kids stay another day. The hotel manager said he'd give us a discount to stay another day.

I called my parents, crying. I told my mom first. She handed the phone over to my dad.

"Dad, I don't know what to do. When I called the principal, he said I have to come home today, or I'm fired. He said he's not going to pay for the hotel, and I can't afford it. And the kids are hungry and don't have anything to wear. They didn't bring money for this. What should I do?"

My dad was furious. "Forget what he thinks. Get the kids some clean T-shirts and underwear with your emergency credit card I gave you and stay an extra day in the hotel. If he has a problem with that, I'll drive down there myself and kick his ass."

I don't remember, but I believe my dad called him…. In any case, we stayed another day. I don't remember if my parents paid for it, or if the school reimbursed them.

The kids and I made the best of the day. We hung out in the hotel room, ate pizza, and just enjoyed watching TV and visiting about the conference. They were donned in oversized white Hanes T-shirts that came in a big bulk pack from Target.

The next day, I white-knuckled the drive home. I felt we were skating down the highway, even though the visibility was better than the previous day. It was still dangerously icy, cold, and windy. We passed abandoned cars in the ditch, frozen monoliths in a world of white. Had we slid off the lonely rural highway, we could have frozen to death. Highway patrol did the best it could to save stranded motorists, but there were no cellphones in those days.

The Tuesday I got back, I tried to avoid the principal, slipping by the office without him seeing me. Later, he cornered me in my library office between classes.

He was furious. I was sitting at my desk in the library office, frozen in fear. As he entered, he slammed the door behind him. His right foot propped itself on my desk and he leaned forward, his crotch inches from my face. I could feel spit landing on my forehead and nose, spewing down, this looming monster over me. I could only stare down at his dirty brown shoe and pukey yellowish-tan pants. Tears welled up in my eyes. I felt frozen, ice cold, and the hair on the back of my neck bristled in fear.

I'd had enough. I was ice cold and shaking in fear as he stomped out of my office and slammed the door loud enough that I knew everyone in the library would be staring. My mind raced. I needed to run away. I needed to hide. I needed to be safe. This treatment wasn't worth any amount of money. I just wanted to be held in my boyfriend's arms, to be safe again.

The head basketball coach heard from outside my library office what had happened. After the principal left, he came in to find me shaking and in tears. Although he hadn't seen the physical aggression, he'd heard bits of the conversation, believed what happened to me, and offered to help get me out of my contract by using a doctor he knew to declare me "suffering from exhaustion."

I went home that day. No one from the school bothered to call me to find out what had happened. I found out later that the previous year a new, young, female teacher had left under mysterious circumstances, supposedly suffering from a nervous breakdown.

After that, I bumped around for a while in my life, broken and crushed that my dream of being a teacher was no more. I started having panic attacks whenever I'd have to walk into a school. This anxiety continued until my own son was in first grade.

My best friend at the time, Lauren, came with me to pick up my things after I left my job. It was extremely difficult, and if she hadn't been there, I don't think I could have done it. She and I have since lost touch, and I miss her so. Lauren, if you are out there, thank you for being a friend to me, when I felt very alone and vulnerable.

The panic attacks ruined my chances of substitute teaching after I left. I really couldn't handle being in a school at all, and loud noises like football games or halftime buzzers still put me over the edge.

I also couldn't handle the pay that teachers were getting where I lived. After quitting teaching, I worked three jobs: retail, janitor at the building where I lived, and a daycare center. I also helped rehab apartments after college students moved out of our rundown, Victorian-style building. It was a way to earn some extra money off my rent. It wasn't a lot of money, but it was more than I had made or saved teaching. By rehabbing apartments, I helped bring up the building's value, and we started getting better quality people in our building—young professionals who were paying higher rent. No more college kids barfing in the stairwells. No more red powder to congeal and harden the vomit so I could sweep it into the dustpan.

No more mice or cockroaches. No more people trashing the laundry room in the basement.

The rehabbing sparked something in me that dogged me until three years ago. Could I make money as an entrepreneur? Because my dad lost his business in the 1980s, it seemed way too scary to try that. Who did I think I was even to consider I could get rich starting my own business?

I did side jobs, even after getting "real" work in document control at a high-tech company. I would help people with résumés, design websites, and continue the janitor and rehabbing work until I moved out of that building.

My boyfriend, who became my husband, transferred to the Bay Area. I fell into a job working in financial services, doing analysis in spreadsheets and databases, crunching numbers, and moving quickly into strategic planning in customer service. I found so many interesting people, with much better Money Messages than I had grown up with.

I even met the founders of Google and their small band of merry musketeers—weird hippy types who were renting space from the firm where I worked. I didn't know Google would become the behemoth it is today, so I passed on an opportunity to work with them. I was afraid to leave a company with a solid paycheck and stock options, even though I thought the other company would be more fun. (Oops.)

Many of my new friends in California saw life as an opportunity, not a struggle. They weren't afraid like I was. Risks were taken for a better life. If you failed, it was just another stepping stone to success.

In the late '90s, venture capitalism and startups were everywhere. There were extravagant parties, people talking about multi-million-dollar deals in the booth behind us at In and Out Burger. It really was the "tech boom." And boy, did I get caught up in it.

Until that bubble burst. Although I'd worked very hard to pay off all my school debt and start a nest egg, everything disappeared quickly, and I had to start over, again.

And again.

And again.

Up to this point, actions spoke louder than words for me. I didn't see these bumps as opportunities. I saw them as failures, and I often made the wrong choices. I was led by fear or insecurity, rather than by logic or a sense of adventure. I would catastrophize the worst and avoid or miss what could have been some of the best parts of my life.

I followed my conditioned pattern, cowering in fear at the prospect of losing something. Instead of figuring out "What is the next step after facing this challenge?" I would get mired in depression.

My Money Message went something like this:

I feel anxiety, depression, or frustration. How can I make it better? I think I'll go hide and eat a pint of Ben and Jerry's Chocolate Cherry Garcia, and maybe it will all go away. I don't care if my bank account is at $15 until Friday. I'll just charge it.

"I realize I'm the one who gave over the power because I didn't know any better. And now that I know better, I know I don't have to do that again. It's one of the most powerful lessons any of us can ever know."

— Oprah Winfrey

When I finally succeeded in taking my wealth management practice independent, I realized that not just one person believed in me, but many people believed in me. It was after my divorce, a point when I didn't even believe in myself. But I knew I had a gift to share, and I was going to try. Maybe it was luck. Maybe it was bootstrapping. Maybe it was a few people who came in and out of my life who taught me valuable lessons. I wish I could put a finger on it to share with you the definitive moment that changed my life, but I can't. It began with one person and trickled from others. It was a gradual shift where I started to have success and realized I didn't have to please anyone else.

As I started living my truth, and sharing that truth, my business grew. As I focused more on the financial lifestyles of my clients, and less on selling product like at my previous firm, I really started examining the Money Messages I had received in the past, and the Money Messages I was receiving and telling myself in the present.

Now it's time for you to do the same. In Part II, you're going to start reflecting on your Money Messages and changing your thoughts about money so you can also pursue the financial lifestyle you want.

PART II
REWRITING YOUR
MONEY MESSAGES

Chapter 8
Understanding Your Money Messages

"Ego says, 'Once everything falls into place, I'll feel peace.'
Spirit says, 'Find your peace, and then everything
will fall into place.'"

— Author Unknown

*N*OW THAT WE'VE LOOKED AT some other people's Money Messages, it's time for us to dive back into your past so you come to a realization about your own. First, you'll need to do some reflection to understand your Money Messages, so we have a place to build from.

REFLECTION AND SOUL SEARCH

What Money Messages did you grow up with?

_____

_____

_____

Money Messages I Learned from My Parents:

_____

_____

_____

Money Messages I Learned from Extended Family:

_____

_____

_____

Money Messages I Learned from Others:

_____

_____

_____

Money Messages That Guide Me:

_____

_____

_____

Money Messages I Wish I Could Change:

_____

_____

_____

What is the biggest Money Message or personal story that holds you back?

_____

_____

_____

What can you do to put this message in the past and move forward?

_____

_____

_____

Is there a specific moment in your life that changed the path of your financial life, for good or bad?

_____

_____

_____

If that specific moment was bad, and it still affects you, what could be the turning point for you in the present?

_____

_____

_____

What kind of support structure can you create—be it tools, people, or something else—to help you with your turning point?

_____

_____

_____

By completing this worksheet, you may have epiphanies, or maybe you will get a small whisper.

Could this be a turning point for you? Are you ready to move forward, beyond what is holding you back?

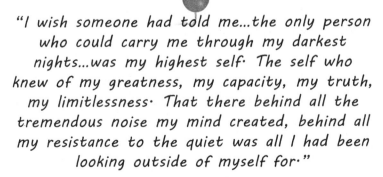

"I wish someone had told me...the only person who could carry me through my darkest nights...was my highest self· The self who knew of my greatness, my capacity, my truth, my limitlessness· That there behind all the tremendous noise my mind created, behind all my resistance to the quiet was all I had been looking outside of myself for."

— Sarah Blondin, *Discovering Your Intrinsic Self*

You are your best source for finding help, and you have three resources, three currencies available to you at any given time, to spend or receive: your time, your skills or talent, and your treasure or physical money.

I once received a gift from my son's godfather. We rarely see each other anymore because we live in different towns and our lives have moved in different directions. However, I still believe he and his wife are two of the most amazing and selfless people I've ever met. They have it figured out. Although they've had several challenges thrown at them over the years, they are disturbingly happy people. They always seem to see the bright side of life.

The gift was Randy Alcorn's book *The Treasure Principle.* Alcorn describes three resources we have or could be short of at any given time: time, talent, and treasure.

And then, we have the messages we tell ourselves about those resources.

Do you ever feel like your time, talent, and treasure are depleted? We probably have no less or no more money, and no less or no more time in a day than we did twenty-four hours ago. We aren't less capable than we were when our head hit the pillow the night before. But it happens...*when we have those days.* The day the car breaks down, and the day the kids are being extra whiny; when work sucks, when time seems short, and when we are unsure what is our purpose in this world except to keep the hamster wheel turning. And we wonder how in the world we will make ends meet?

The messages you tell yourself about your wealth are the most important component when it comes to building your life. The Money Messages you have running inside of your head influence how you think and feel about money.

> Ask yourself,
> "How are my Money Messages helping or hurting me?"

I don't know if there is such a thing as false beliefs when it comes to money and Money Messages. That's because the person who believes the message feels the message resonate from within them, or feels the message from the outside trigger them. The Money Message *feels* true for that person. However, I do believe some messages limit potential, and if we can recognize when those messages are dominating, we can catch them and turn things around.

Constructive Money Messages open potential. And the good news is: This can all be learned!

Obviously, some things are beyond your control. I can't always prevent my car from breaking down. I can't control if my partner or child is in a bad mood. But I can bring my frequency to a higher level and focus on what I *can* do.

What can I control? I can control my work effort. I can take things day by day, and realize bumps in the road may come, but I am the master of my little universe at least for this present moment.

I am the master of my attitude. I could kick my car, and scream, and pull my hair, but what does that solve?

When I got a flat tire while transporting a student home after a volunteer event, I could have become really upset and started crying. Instead, I laughed with the student and said, "Watch this." I changed and put on the spare tire myself. Not only did he laugh and say he had a good story to tell, but we got back on the road a lot faster than if I'd had a temper tantrum about it. And, I modeled good behavior for that student.

When we do lose our shit—and it happens to all of us—it's important that we are kind, forgive ourselves, and figure out how to move forward. Putting things into perspective, we can realize that a bad day, or even a tragic situation, doesn't have to dictate every day and how one feels until infinity and beyond.

I recently interviewed Linda Conroy, a nationally respected herb-alist and the founder of the Midwest Women's Herbal Conference. Linda grew up in a small, Italian neighborhood outside of Philadel-phia. Her father went to art school and became a photographer. Her mother was an entrepreneur with several businesses over the years.

"My parents didn't have a lot of money," Linda told me, "but it's what they did, and this had a huge impact on me as an adult: they pursued their dreams. That was the priority—that there was pas-sion—and somehow trusting the resources and that your basic needs will always be taken care of."

The message of "passion before money" was something Linda be-came grateful for. She believes that Money Message from her parents allowed her to have less attachment to material things and a greater focus on experiences that mattered to her. "I never said to myself, 'I'm going to have this much money before I would take a risk.' I take a lot of risks in pursuing what is important to me and what matters."

Linda believes many people have a sense of "lack" when it comes to money. Money becomes a trigger of pain and confusion for them, especially women.

"I've certainly grappled with a lot of different things over the years, that's for sure," Linda shared. "I personally live very modestly, but I certainly have visions of a culture that is richer in other things."

I often speak of money as an exchange of energy. Linda defines it as an exchange of power:

> Money is simply a tool. Think about debt. Every time you use your credit card, you're giving your power away and someone else is taking that power with the high interest rates. So, if you have that power to yourself—and you're able to manifest what you need in your life within the means that you have, and not borrow somebody else's means—that is more power or energy you can save for yourself and then share with others. I

predominantly work with women, and women certainly don't have a sense that they—I don't like the word "deserve"—but they don't have a sense that they have the right to have enough money—to be cared for. Women have a sense of taking care of other people before themselves, and that comes into play a lot of times when it comes to negotiating and dealing with finances.

When I first met Linda, I was going through a transition. My divorce was final, and I had just launched my own venture. My stress level was high, and I was at rock bottom emotionally. During a moment at the Midwest Women's Herbal Conference, I shared my fears and uncertainties with her. I told her how the "I can't" theme was going through my mind.

Then I mentioned that I was frustrated with the free consulting I was doing to try to win new clients.

Linda nearly yelled at me.

"THEN WHY ARE YOU DOING THAT? You should charge for your services."

I hemmed and hawed. I explained that I had just come from a brokerage firm where we didn't charge for advice.

"Excuses, excuses," she said. "Don't compromise your worth. Be proud of what you do."

I remained quiet as she gave me advice. Internally, I was kicking and screaming like a two-year old. I felt anger bubbling up. *How dare she tell me what to do with my business?*

But her words made an impact. This "wise woman," my mentor, had given me tough mother love mixed with encouragement. Even in my anger, I remember seeing an aura coming off her, which shone like a bright light. This woman had the power of *presence* about her.

After thinking it over, I realized she wanted the best for me. Her perspective brought me back home to myself. Her advice quieted the ten thousand squirrels squeaking, "I can't."

I thought, *If she could do it, and she told me I can do it, I will!*

I decided to take Linda's advice to charge what I was worth and to really embrace who I was as a person. After I talked to my firm, we created an hourly financial planning contract I could use in those situations where the client didn't have assets to manage or didn't want me to manage investments but simply wanted my planning services. I didn't have to give away my time anymore, and this simple practice elevated my feelings about my work's value.

I had to learn to stop saying, "I can't," and shift to "I can." I had to decide what my next step would be, and how to climb over that mountain in my path. It had nothing to do with my potential, or what anyone else believed I could or couldn't do.

I had to decide what I was worth.

That simple mindset shift also shifted my own Money Message and the actions that followed. Within a year, I transitioned my practice and flourished. Today, just over four years later, I am a partner at the firm.

REFLECTION AND SOUL SEARCH

The next exercise requires some vulnerability. I want you to take a moment to consider the following questions and answer each of them *honestly*.

What kind of saver or spender are you?

_____

_____

_____

Do you binge or purge to your detriment in your financial life? What triggers a binge/purge?

Do you self-sabotage your financial goals when you start making some financial gains?

Is money a sticking point that affects your relationships with your spouse, parents, children, or friends?

Do you get wrapped up and stressed by day-to-day news of the stock market?

Do you know what you need to do to make your financial life better, but feel paralyzed or stuck, and can't seem to start?

Are you currently saving in your work retirement plan, and outside your retirement plan?

How much money do you have saved for a rainy day? This is called an *emergency fund.*

_____

_____

_____

Do you look at your work as something you need to suffer through for a distant pot of gold called "retirement"?

_____

_____

_____

Do you think of your job as something that excites you and you wouldn't mind doing as long as you are physically able?

_____

_____

_____

Do you believe one of the following? Monetary wealth is a) "the root of all evil," b) a tool, c) a dream someone else can achieve but not you, or d) something else, good or bad?

_____

_____

_____

How did your parents feel about money? Do you feel differently or the same, and why?

_____

_____

_____

Do you feel threatened, shut down, jealous, embarrassed, angry, or by contrast, curious, indifferent, or excited when the subject of money comes up in social interactions?

_____

_____

_____

Do you know your credit score?

_____

_____

_____

Do you track your finances?

_____

_____

_____

Look within to understand your responses. When I ask people these questions, I sometimes hear a shy, "I don't know." Sometimes I hear stories; I hear people reliving memories of where these thoughts came from. For some individuals, it's almost as though I'm reliving a traumatic situation with them. These stories are not just messages from the past...that stay in the past. These messages are still very much alive, present, and sitting next to us. Until we can identify the shadows that frequent our restless nights, we can't release those stories.

Valuing Yourself, Not Your Possessions

Regardless of how you do it, find ways to value yourself beyond possessions and social trappings. If you have the feeling you are worth it, you won't need money and status spending to feel "worth it."

> *"People don't buy for logical reasons. They buy for emotional reasons."*
>
> — Zig Ziglar

I read a few articles recently about Marilyn Manson, shock-rocker and flaunter of physical and monetary excesses. (He often uses his performance art in a satirical way.) Born Brian Warner, he encountered many traumas as a kid, and more once he became famous. In the last couple of years, increasingly erratic behavior has been reported. He has been haunted since the Columbine school shooting by the unfair accusations of culpability—of being directly responsible for the shooters. The deep dark hole of trauma, and dwelling in it, is addictive. Our caveman brains are constantly in search of fight or flight to fend off saber-toothed tigers. What happens if there are no saber-toothed tigers? Our brain will subconsciously create the monster. I'm not saying Marilyn Manson is running from imaginary monsters, and I am not his therapist, but how long can someone live in a dark hole without being able to crawl out of it?

In recovering from my own traumas, I have used various methods: therapy, yoga, running, and meditation. Financially, I turned away from a spending addiction to filling my emotional void by only using a debit card.

In our daily practice, how can we turn to presence, intentionality, and peace to improve both our personal and financial lives? Can you list yours?

Drawing upon Melissa Ambrosini's book *Mastering Your Mean Girl*, let's have a conversation with your mean girl or boy. We'll go into the hole for a moment, and then we'll rediscover ourselves as our own best friends and pull ourselves out. First, I'd like you to ponder all those horrible things you tell yourself about relationships or money.

Do any of these resonate with you?

- "I'm ugly."
- "I'm fat."
- "Who would possibly love a loser like me?"
- "I'm in such a financial hole that there's no way out."
- "I suck with money."
- "Why do I keep picking the wrong partner?"

REFLECTION AND SOUL SEARCH

Write down any horrible sayings that resonate with you or that you find yourself saying to yourself. We'll figure out a new way to talk to yourself in the next section.

_____

_____

_____

_____

_____

_____

A New Way to Talk to Yourself

I was fortunate to experience a "Shadow Work" session with ALisa Starkweather at the Midwest Women's Herbal Conference, run by Linda Conroy, whom I mentioned earlier. ALisa (that's not a typo; that's how she spells her name) is the founder of many powerful women's initiatives, including the Red Tent Temple Movement, Daughters of the Earth Gatherings, and the Women's Belly and Womb Conferences. She is also a Shadow Work and Breathwork facilitator, keynote speaker, and life coach. She is well known for her passionate archetypal work that focuses on transformation, healing, community, ritual, and rebalancing the sacred feminine.

I joined ALisa's session at the pre-conference on an overcast day—a perfectly gloomy atmosphere to wallow in depression and sadness. I was feeling pretty blue. I hoped the conference would give me some hope, strength, and sisterhood.

As I sat in a circle with the other attendees—all strangers—ALisa asked us to stand. She had us face outwards from the circle so we couldn't see each other. We were each handed a totem: a faceless, cloth-rag doll. We were instructed to talk silently to the doll.

First, we held the doll at our waist, looking at it, and dreamed up all the horrible things we could say to this doll like we would during our worst moments with ourselves.

The world went a bit fuzzy around me as I focused on the doll. I had a lot of mean things to say to myself. Tears streamed down my cheeks. Time passed slowly. It was a discomfort that felt like forever, though it was perhaps only a few minutes.

Then, ALisa asked us to put the doll on our chair and turn around to face one another. She asked us to hold hands and sit in silence together. As we gazed at each other, all of us had red, muddled faces streaked with tears. She asked rhetorically if we would say any of those words to each other.

> "Would you intentionally make another person hurt,
> the way you are hurting right now?"

Several of us shook our heads in a silent "no," and some of us even sobbed. ALisa spoke of love, light, and rising above. Her words flowed through the air, intermingling with the shuffling of campers arriving and walking past our tent. I was conscious of some of the campers staring at our group, all teary faced. However, a sense of bonding was already coming over us, and we felt safe…. ALisa held a safe space for us, and we for each other in that shadowed tent. We discovered our inner child who had internalized the words of cruelty we had no doubt heard from others. She shared with us that children are not naturally born with these feelings of insecurity. Someone else said those words to us, just as we said them to the doll.

Our hands tightened, holding each other up, and holding our circle together. ALisa asked us to have kind thoughts for our sisters in the circle who were in pain. Then, she asked us to turn to our chairs. She asked us to look at the doll. She asked us to talk once again to the doll, this time as if it were an innocent child and we were the adults.

Everything shifted. I imagined this doll as the child version of my-self.... Some of us hugged our dolls. I held her up into the light and smiled gently at her. Then, I held the doll close and comforted her, telling her how I felt about her, how special she was, and how loved she was.

We came out of the tent together. Then picking up imaginary bows and arrows, we aimed them to the sky. ALisa told us to release the pain, to let it fly away into the air, and to step into the light, into the people we were meant to be.

When you find yourself saying those mean things to yourself that you'd never say to another, use this exercise to shift your messages to yourself. The words we choose have tremendous impact.

Chapter 9
Your Circumstances and Your Choices

*"The first step of change is to become aware
of your own bullshit."*

— Author Unknown

I OFTEN LISTEN TO PODCASTS OR audiobooks. One certainty in Chicago is traffic, so while driving from appointment to appointment, or to my office, great storytellers help me enjoyably float through what most people would consider dreadful commutes. Time is also part of wealth, and this little practice of listening to something enjoyable and educational while driving helps me reclaim some of that gift of time, instead of succumbing to frustration or road rage.

Recently, I was speaking with another business owner, a lawyer friend of mine, who also loves listening to good podcasts while she commutes. She referred me to a podcast series called *The Dream*, hosted by Jane Marie.

One story in the series really caught my attention. I had to find out more about it, and scoured Wikipedia, YouTube, and other online sites for more information about this story. In the early 1960s, William Penn Patrick was down on his luck. He had the idea for a business scheme, but he didn't have the right product. He was passing by a garage in San Rafael, California, when he smelled the most amazing fruit scent wafting through the neighborhood. He walked in and discovered a company, Zolene, making fruit-scented cosmetics. He bought the company, and Holiday Magic, a fruit-scented cosmetics titan, was born. By age thirty-four, Patrick was a millionaire, and by thirty-six, he was a multi-millionaire, according to a *New York Times* article published February 19, 1973.

Yet, by 1973, at age forty-three, William's world was caving in on him. The thing is the product was not what was creating the profits—his business was built on a shaky foundation.

Mr. Patrick recruited "distributors" to buy in to the business to sell his cosmetics, and they would, in turn, get paid for anyone they recruited. He used these distributorships to create what we now know as a "pyramid scheme." He was able to get his distributors to do unthinkable things because they were brainwashed into his mind dynamics techniques—things that had nothing to do with scented cosmetics. He tested their loyalty and level of brainwashing by using peer pressure and crowd bullying tactics. He created shocking practices to make these distributors show their loyalty by hanging on crosses and lying in closed coffins! Isn't that crazy? Why would any sane person do that? How could one man be so evil, yet so self-righteous in his pursuit of personal wealth?

As humans, it's easier to fall for false promises or peer pressure than one would think....

How often do you hear about something that seems too good to be true? You know them—those "As Seen on TV" infomercials that promise youth, unlimited wealth, happiness...if...only...you...buy in!

How often do we "buy in" to things we know will not help us, but we fall for the false promises anyway? Others tell us that if we think a certain way, do a certain thing, or buy a certain product, it will make us happy—so we go for it, despite our common sense telling us otherwise.

I just recently bought a hair-extension accessory that looked great in the videos. I envisioned beautiful waves cascading down my shoulders, just as the video promised, but the product is now hanging uselessly on the back hook of my makeup table, like a dead ferret.

I could probably return it, but instead, it will serve as a reminder that I wasted $30. But...it was only $30, right? There is a term for this thought process. It's called "writing off losses." It's easy for us to spend money on something, and actually end up paying more than a small sum, only to be disappointed.

Why did I buy that stupid hair extension?

Because someone had made a critical remark about how I looked the week before, and I saw it, and thought, "Ooh, that might make me look prettier."

Instead, I should have told myself, "Well, that's just one person's opinion. My husband thinks I'm beautiful, and I like the way I look most of the time, so why should it matter?"

Think about the little app on your phone; you started paying $2 a month, or maybe nothing, for the introductory subscription. Then, after the trial period ended, it went up to $69...not because you want it, or have even used it since the day you bought in, but because you forgot to cancel it. You shrug, and maybe you then call the company to cancel. Or not.

Companies count on this "writing off losses" mentality to make extra money from you that you did not intend to spend. In our PayPal, Amazon, and Apple Pay world, corporations depend on the impulse buyer clicking, and if there's buyer's remorse later, the consumer probably won't cause a fuss or go through the trouble to return the product or cancel the service. Maybe the seller has made it too difficult, or downright impossible, to get your money back.

But let's go back to multi-level marketing for a moment. *The Dream* claims a higher prevalence of these schemes exists in more economically depressed areas. And these types of companies traditionally use women to market their products. A friend of the program's narrator is one of the top salespeople in the country for a particular product and has a huge downline of over 280 other sellers, yet she makes a mere $42,000 a year. If you live in an economically depressed area, or if you are a stay-at-home mom with few opportunities, $42,000 is a lot of money.

Most of the time, however, regardless of what product you sell, if you are in a multi-level marketing company, your average annual profit will be much less than $42,000, and most of your money will not come from selling product, but from recruiting other distributors. And when the well runs dry, and your friends start avoiding you at church or the swimming pool, you will know this is not what you signed up for.

False Promises

In our emotional arsenal of positive Money Messages, if we are satisfied with our life and lifestyle, we are less likely to fall for false promises. I propose that people in a more emotional (or real) economically challenged position are more likely to give in to false promises, because when you don't have money, hope is what you must rely on. The podcast I listened to talked about "overweighting small probability events." If you are feeling like things haven't been going well financially, are you more or less likely to buy a lottery ticket? Are you more or less likely to impulse buy something to make you feel better?

You may feel good for a moment, imagining how this ticket will be the winner, or how that product will answer your prayers and take away the bad feelings, but it will only last a few minutes to a few days.

Just like any other addiction, overspending to fill a void is "consumer addiction." If you are in a bad place about your money, your looks, or your family, you may decide to buy things to fill the void, to take away the pain.

Status Spending

Have you had issues with binge spending, or buying things you realize you didn't need? If you feel bad enough emotionally, you may look at others and become jealous. Why does she have a nice car when I'm driving a ten-year-old junker? Why does Jason post a zillion Instagram or Facebook pictures of his lovely cabin in the woods, while I'm here at home procrastinating on mowing my lawn because I can't even afford a lawn-mowing service?

Again, check in with the Money Messages. How can you flip the script? Can you turn around the thought to gratitude? *I have a car. I own a beautiful house with a lovely yard. I own a lawn mower and it's a beautiful day to be outside.*

If you are living in *true poverty*, or a truly horrible environment, it's time to refer to Chapter 1: Taking Charge of Your Destiny. *What are you doing with your life?* How can you move out of this?

It's time to release any toxic situations or environments. If you need to escape an abusive situation, geographic location, personal addiction, or something that damaged your soul, *you* need to make the decision to:

1. Get help

2. Get out, and

3. *Move Forward.*

Life will never be the same. It will be tempting to jump back into the pit of hopelessness, but you can transform your life! It won't be easy, but you can do it. There are so many resources out there for you. Do an internet search on terms like human services, homelessness, abuse/addiction/whatever support, and your county and state. You will find something to give you a start. Unlike previous generations, we can evolve beyond our societal limitations because the world is changing, and help is at our fingertips with the wonders of the internet and our increasingly global world. Supportive communities, be they real or virtual, exist for almost any population, and are at the ready to help you beyond your situation and beyond your geographic location. So many non-profit support organizations are out there; you just need to find them!

If you forget your path and start worrying about the loved ones you may affect, or that you might hurt someone as you transform your life—remember the pre-flight announcement:

> In the event of a decompression, an oxygen mask will automatically appear in front of you. [Take action.] To start the flow of oxygen, pull the mask towards you. Place it firmly over your nose and mouth, secure the elastic band behind your head, and breathe normally. [Breathe.] Although the bag does not inflate, oxygen is flowing to the mask. [Focus on what you can control.] If you are traveling with a child or someone who requires assistance, secure your mask first, and then assist the other person. [You can't help others if you don't help yourself first.]

Rising Above Your Circumstances

Jade Carpenter is known by many in my community. She is a stunningly beautiful person, both inside and out. She is also a force to be reckoned with as a corporate and personal lawyer. Most people don't know her story.

Jade's dad's side of the family was economically stable, and her early childhood included a nice big home, a pond, and an acre of land in

Pickerington, Ohio. Then her parents fell into alcohol and drug addiction. They both lost their jobs. By the time Jade was eleven, her family had moved to a small two-bedroom trailer in Lancaster, Ohio. A year later, Jade's mother passed away. Jade ended up with her aunt and uncle in Indiana and fell into the pit of her circumstances. "I ended up getting into drugs myself," she told me. "We liked to go to hookah bars. I got into a lot of trouble and got expelled from school. I ended up in juvenile detention because of my drug use, running away, and being with the wrong people. Then I ended up on probation, in foster care, and Alcoholics Anonymous."

Then, she got shot in the head. "It was the summer before my senior year of high school, Father's Day. My dad was incarcerated, and I went to visit him that day, and then I went downtown with my friends. We were in a Taco Bell parking lot right by the OSU campus. There was a big group of bikers, like motorcycle riders, and we were just talking with them. I didn't really know any of these people."

Despite the unpleasant experience of visiting her dad in jail, it was a beautiful summer night, and Jade was enjoying herself, visiting with her friends and the bikers. She later learned that one guy had a history with three other guys who saw him parked outside. The three men left, got guns, and the driver put on a bulletproof vest. They came back to the parking lot and shot into the crowd. Jade was the first person hit. The bullet entered the left side by her neck, went through her face, and came out underneath her right eye. It was a 45-hollow point—a big bullet—and tore off much of her face.

"I only have like two split second memories from the evening because I went into shock. But I just remember at one point sitting on the ground. I'm just thinking something really serious had happened and I needed to just keep breathing, essentially. And then I remember being put into the ambulance and that they were taking my purse from me. Other than that, I remember waking up in the hospital. My friends have a few different accounts of what happened. My friend

Jessica was there; she thought I had got shot in the arm and the leg, which I did not at all. I guess there was just so much blood. She didn't even know where I'd gotten shot, so it was wild. They actually had to call and get permission from my dad. They had to get my dad on the phone at the jail to get permission to do surgery. He told me he thought it was a car accident and he never would have thought I had gotten shot.

"Thankfully, there were amazing, amazing surgeons who lifted my face off of my skull, took out bone fragments, and put plates in. I was wired shut, and I had a trake and a feeding tube. I was in the hospital for about five days. Then I went to stay with an aunt who, thankfully, is an RN and took care of me."

Jade experienced an outpouring of support. After that, Jade's life began to change for the better. When I asked her what turned her life around from the hookah bar, trouble-making teen, she couldn't directly name a specific moment. However, having a support system definitely helped.

"It was pretty amazing," Jade said, "because even the vice principal from my high school, she came and we did a custody schedule for me so I could get out of school early because school was starting, I think a month later." With Jade's injuries, the vice principal thought it was a lot for her to try to do a whole day. Jade persevered. "I was able to go back to school on time and, even with everything going on, I've always done really well in school. I've always been on the honor roll and I've always loved school, even though I was, you know, getting into trouble. I actually was able to be the senior speaker at graduation, which was a lot of fun. After that, I just went right to college, which I did my first year down in South Carolina."

Jade knew that staying in her current environment wouldn't be healthy for her, and she wanted to see the world. She also knew she needed to safeguard her finances because she didn't want to end up like her parents and lose everything. She was lucky to find funding for her education, but she's had to work and save to become financially stable. She said she is pretty conservative in her finances, but she still looks for experiences where she can travel. She decided to pursue law because she wanted to be an advocate for other people stuck in the legal system like she was when she was in foster care. "I have seen quite a few places. I just knew I wanted to leave Ohio [after high school]. So that was my one goal. And then, you know, obviously I applied for financial aid, which I think I got a little more because I was a ward of the state from when I was in foster care. So that was [more] helpful than just scholarships. My family had put together a college fund for me, too, so that helped."

Jade knows these gifts gave her an advantage, and she's grateful for the opportunities she had in pursuing her education. She also interned for a lawyer who led her to her current career as an attorney in independent practice. "You know, a lot of people I ran with when I was getting into trouble are either dead or did not get a college education or are in much different situations than I am. I think that was one of the big differences—that I had that college fund." A little bit of the rebel remains, and in an interview with CBS news, Jade recounted getting a tattoo of "3%" behind her ear where the bullet entered her head, "because 20,000 Americans are shot in the head each year, but only 3 percent get their lives back. 'I'm one of those 3 percent that lived, and I have a great quality of life now.'"

Jade encourages other people who have faced difficult circumstances to persevere in pursuing education as a means to success. "If I wouldn't have gone, I probably would not be a lawyer. I might not be alive. There are options. A majority of my colleagues I went to law school with have six figure debt, and it sucks, and it's something they'll probably have for the rest of their lives. Yet, people are making it work. They have successful jobs, they're succeeding, they're happy. They're still able to get mortgages to buy homes if they need to."

Jade doesn't believe, with all that she's been through, that any situation is impossible: "Things always get better, period. That's just what I've experienced in life. Even with everything that I've been through in my life—lost my parents, gone to jail, been shot, plenty of things. I'm only twenty-seven, but it's all been character building." It has now been ten years since that fateful day. Jade strongly believes life's difficulties make us stronger. "It really makes you stronger. And so, the next thing that comes, you can handle it even better, but it just always gets better. It's not always bad, and it's all about how you approach it. It can either make you or break you. You can let it build you. You can learn from it. You can grow from it, or you can, you know, let it tear you down."

Jade acknowledges it's not always easy. She shares that we all have moments of vulnerability:

> It's hard sometimes to approach things with a positive mentality. Things can happen in life that are outside of your control, but how you deal with it is within your control. I think sometimes people dwell on the past or what's going on—things they can't change. It's important to just focus on the things you can change. And that's what's always gotten me through. I can focus on all the people who are good in my life now. I won't lie; I even have nightmares sometimes that I'm back in jail and I'm like, 'No, I'm good now.' I've sought out therapy, but I don't, you know, it's not—it hasn't been my thing, but it completely works for other people. I focus on how I've been able to build my life and how happy I am and how good my life is.... I am grateful every day.... It keeps me from backsliding. I have a home, I have a partner, and I have a good job. I've made it, and I did it! I'm just grateful for where I am, and I want to continue to build. I only want to go up from here, and that's what keeps me moving forward.

I'll write myself notes like, 'You survived this and can continue to survive anything.' I let it boost my self-esteem. When we have trauma, it can haunt us. Or we can be like, 'You know what? I survived that! I'm going to survive the next thing too.' [The notes] kind of remind me that I'm pretty badass.

What an amazing story! As a financial advisor, I have met amazing men and women of different backgrounds who have overcome many forms of lack and become successful. I can never completely understand the challenges some of my friends face in my beloved South Side Chicago, or what Jade went through coming from parental neglect, personal drug addiction, and being shot. I can't answer for every situation of lack of opportunity, but I can relate to being held back and abused professionally and personally as a woman.

I love the well-known proverb:

> *"The best revenge is a life well lived."*

Your abusers, if you are a victim of abuse, don't give two wags of a tail about you. I'm sorry; it's harsh, but it's true. I'm way beyond waiting for an apology from anyone. Like Jade, I've had to confront my own personal demons and get past myself as a barrier to my own success. Nicki Minaj, for all her wild antics, has the best quote, "You're not going to tell me who I am; I'm going to tell you who I am."

Racism is not going away. Sexism is not going away. Homophobia is not going away. Abusive environments are not going away. Abject poverty is not going away. But there comes a point when you have to say, "This is not my story anymore. I am a beautiful person, not a label, and I will no longer let the criticisms of anyone, real or imagined, past or present, hold power over me and I will…move…forward."

Believe me when I shake you by the shoulders and say, "There is another way, if you find what you are talented at, or what you could be talented at, and *go for it!*" You are one in 400 trillion. You may not have treasure right now, but you need to make the time, and you certainly have a talent, or you can develop a talent. Find your professional or personal resources and speak with them about your situation. Find out *not* what can they give you, but what you can do to ameliorate your situation for yourself now and going forward.

Do you need to go back to school and learn a different skill set? Do you need to move to a different area? Is your spending for your dwelling too high for the amount of money you are making? (In our financial planning classes, we learn that no more than 28 percent of your money should go to housing. Did you know that, by law, lenders can't approve mortgages that are higher than 35 percent of your household income?)

You need to be willing to:

1. Take accountability and look at your situation. Being in poverty or debt may or may not have been your fault but recognize the areas you can control or improve to move forward.
2. Remember that the past is now past, and you could change your situation, or your perception of the situation now, and move forward.
3. Realize you have choices.

I am here to tell you nothing is impossible, unless you have decided it is impossible.

Whether you are living in poverty, living beyond your means, or just miserable and stuck in a rut, something needs to change. And you will be the one to change it.

The inscription on the Seabees Memorial in Washington, DC still rings true today, "With willing hearts and skillful hands, the difficult we do at once; the impossible takes a bit longer."

REFLECTION AND SOUL SEARCH

What circumstances are holding you back financially and from pursuing your full potential?

_____

_____

_____

_____

What financial changes can you begin to make today?

_____

_____

_____

_____

Do you need to change your living situation? List five options you have.

_____

_____

_____

_____

_____

List in order the first five actions you need to take to improve your circumstances. Beside each one list a date that you promise yourself you will take action by. You wouldn't break a promise to someone else, so don't break it to yourself.

Action   Date to Take

1. _____

2. _____

3. _____

4. _____

5. _____

The Power of Giving

Brett Weiss and I have gotten to know one another over the years through Rotary. What an amazing person he is! He was a successful high school teacher who "retired," and decided to take his mission to the world, funding children to attend schools in Kenya. He has since devoted his life to creating opportunities for Kenyan children, and he is the author of *Just Give Them a Hug...and the Rest Will Be Easy: How One Person Can Make the World a Better Place, One Child at a Time.*

It didn't start out that way. It started with one trip, and one life shift.

In 2009, Brett took a trip to Dago, Kenya, with the group Village Volunteers. There, he encountered a young boy who started sobbing.

Brett asked the boy what was wrong. Through an interpreter, the boy explained that he had broken his pencil, so now he wouldn't be able to do his lessons.

Brett pulled out a pen and handed it to the boy.

You would have thought it was the Holy Grail. The boy was so grateful.

Brett's only regret was that he didn't have pencils and pencil sharpeners to give the kids, which would have had a more sustaining effect on their lives.

Well, Brett went home and gathered as many pencils and sharpeners as he could find. He returned to Dago with pencils and pencil sharpeners.

And Brett went back many times. He started a foundation helping schools and creating scholarships for students. Brett has changed hundreds, if not thousands, of lives. This man is on fire, and nothing stops him from sharing his message and raising money for his foundation.

What is Brett's "why"?

"At the end of my life," he wrote in his book, "I did not want to look back at a list of things I had wanted to do but didn't because I kept coming up with weak excuses."

When I asked Brett about the Money Messages he grew up with, he shared:

> For me it starts with my parents who were Depression babies. My dad had his own business, and while we were not wealthy, we always had a nice life. My parents taught us to always be trying to help those not as blessed as we were. Any time we help someone in need, that is a great thing. But (and I know there are many quotes that say something like this) the best kind of giving is to give to someone who can never pay you back. The children we help can give us nothing back in a material sense. Also, as I have grown older, I really enjoy helping children, even though most of the benefits they will get from their education will come after my time on earth is over.
>
> I am a big believer in living simply. (Mother Teresa said, "Live simply so others may simply live.") In our world, we have an overabundance of so much. Most Americans can just take a little of this overabundance and it will do a great deal to help a poor child, and in reality, will have no real impact on their own lives.
>
> Also, since education has been much of my life, I am passionate about it. While people in Third World countries need everything (food, medical, water, housing, electricity, plumbing, etc.), the only long-term and sustainable solution to poverty is getting children a great education. Education is the answer that solves all the other questions.

My favorite part of this is when I visit our kids at their boarding high school. I do these video interviews, and at times, I am in tears. These kids are so appreciative of the opportunity they have been given because they know most of the children they grew up with are back in the village and their lives will not be any different. Also, each of these children has a passion to help others the way they have been helped. They are very committed to helping their family and others back in the village.

I have two little grandkids now whom I really enjoy. When I look at them, I think about how I want to do everything I can to help as many little children in Kenya to have a great life.

I guess most important is it has made me appreciate my life and all the blessings I have had a lot more. I deal with people in Kenya who really have nothing in terms of material things, but they are the nicest, kindest, and hardest working people I have ever met. They really do not complain. They just get up every day and make the best of it, and almost always with a big smile. It has made me realize that most of the things I worry about are just a waste of time. I have learned I really have very little to worry about.

To learn more about Brett and his amazing work, visit him at www.WeissScholarshipFoundation.org.

You can do whatever you set your mind to if you go at it with a heart of gratitude for life right now, and an idea and plan for the future.

If the junker car doesn't work for you, start saving for a better car. And when you get that new car, keep that savings fund going so you won't have to make as big a sacrifice five years down the road when the shiny new car becomes the next piece of junk.

Instant gratification is fleeting. There is always a price to pay, and it's usually higher than if you could just wait and do it the more prudent way. Gratification with material things is always fleeting. Knowing in your heart that you are a good person and you are doing the best you can will help you make better decisions as time goes on.

People can debate all day long on the benefits of leveraging, or what is or is not wasteful spending, but if you are leveraging on things that have no hope of increasing in value, it's not leveraging. It's debt. Who do you want to give your power to? Yourself, or a credit card company/debt corporation? Do you empower yourself to be the very best you can be? Do you share your time, your skills, or your wealth to empower others to be their best?

"There is freedom waiting for you,
On the breezes of the sky,
And you ask, 'What if I fall?'
Oh, but my darling,
What if you fly?"
— Erin Hanson

Chapter 10
Love and Money Messages:
Finding Financial Compatibility

"A first date question: How aware are you of your traumas
& suppressed emotions and tell me about how you are
actively working to heal them before you try to
project that shit on me?"

— WildWomanSisterhood.com

I REGRET TO SAY I AM divorced from my son's father. I am protective and private about most of it. Both of us are good people, we made a wonderful kid together, and we both moved on with our lives.

But I will tell you this: It took me several years of therapy to realize we both had traumas in our past we had not resolved, and the aftermath played itself out in many wars, including money wars—vacations not in the budget, impulse purchases we couldn't afford. We used money on one side to fill the empty hole in our relationship, to replace the love we were losing for each other. On the other side, we used money as a passive-aggressive way to dig under each other's skin when we were upset with each other. We were both guilty, and I, at least, now realize my culpability in the marriage breakdown. Money was at the center of many of our issues, and it played out in a tug of war over "I want" and "No, you can't."

Since coming to this realization, I've worked hard to make amends to my broken spirit. I fixed my spending habits, started saving, and became debt free.

Money was still tight right after my divorce, but I identified and healed many of my Money Messages and created a much healthier money story about who I am and who I want to be going forward. I started to heal past traumas around money and around love. I decided if there wasn't someone who could share my values about money and commitment, saving and spending, I would rather be alone, just me and my son, against the world.

After several dating experiences, I began to realize you cannot change another person. You cannot rescue a person. *You only have a choice about your own behavior now and going forward.* I also realized it's necessary to clearly communicate who you are and what you want, and not to compromise your thoughts and beliefs to what you think the other person wants to hear. You must stand your ground and be strong in communicating your needs. It's ironic that the digital society that has helped us become global citizens can also plunge us into isolation and loneliness. I think many of us, both men and women, are so desperate to be loved in this increasingly disconnected electronic society that we will say and do things not in alignment with who we really are.

That said, I did find my current husband through an online dating site. Recently, another business professional, who also found her husband online, and I were giving another over-forty girlfriend some advice on online dating. I'll share a bit of this discussion here because the Money Messages and personal self-esteem we have, or don't have, plays out in the microcosm of dating more strongly than anywhere else in the human experience. Here's the advice we shared:

- Know thyself. Be uncompromisingly you.

- Realize that who you are is who you are going to attract.

- You may also attract a predator who will manipulate your goodwill. Beware, and do not suffer fools.

- Have honest conversations about money in the dating stages. You would not accept a new job without knowing your financial potential there (at least I hope not), so why would you allow a partner to be in your life long-term without knowing where they stand?

- Do not let love, lust, or loneliness cloud your striving for compatibility and honesty in all matters, including money matters.

- Money issues are the number one reason for divorce, followed by infidelity.

- Infidelity demonstrates a lack of honesty on a personal love level. If there is dishonesty in one of the most intimate areas of your relationship—sex and personal intimacy—how easily could this betrayal cross over into your money story with your partner?

After my divorce, I healed well financially, but I would be lying if I said I was completely healed personally before I met my current husband. I have sometimes clung to toxic relationships to try to "prove myself." Time, experience, and lots of life coaching and therapy have helped. I am getting better at not tolerating people who treat me as "little" or "less than." If I allow myself to believe I have no worth, then money has no worth, and I could fall back into that cycle of binge spending.

If we are who we are meant to be, there is no risk in asking for what we deserve. After much self-work, I revised my dating profile. I had healed enough to know very distinctly who and what I wanted in my future partner. I deleted many messages and blocked many users without responding. I owed them nothing. They owed me nothing, and I didn't obsess if I sent a message to someone who looked interesting, but I received no response. I focused more on the relationships that mattered most to me—the biggest loves of my life: myself and my son. We went for walks. We sat together while he did homework. We did movie nights, made tent forts, and shared those last minutes of magic before he grew up to be the pre-teen I know today. I am so thankful for that time, every single minute. And I am humbled by the amazing man he is becoming.

I am blessed, but if I had not taken the risk to become who I was meant to be, if I had not been insistent on what I wanted and needed in a relationship, including open dialogue about finances, my life would not be as full and amazing as it is today.

I stopped worrying whether a man loved me or not as a definition of my personal value. I became comfortable with being alone and being a single parent. Clients who judged me for my divorce were left behind. I wanted to surround myself with positive people I could cheerlead, and who would inspire me. As my business has grown, I have worked with more and more entrepreneurs, and they fascinate me.

Entrepreneurs, or people with entrepreneurial leverage in their company, more than any group of people, have taken a big step toward recognizing what they want in life. In essence, they have done a dating profile with their career, and seek freedom in their time, maximizing the use of their talents, and have great potential for creating wealth. Business owners have also taken personal ownership of their careers rather than being subject to the whims of an employer who could dismiss them. "At will employment" usually means, "You will be my employee as long as I like you, you are doing something for me, and I can afford you. Otherwise, to quote a certain man, 'You're fired!'" Do we sometimes find that same attitude in bad love relationships?

So, let's be the entrepreneur of our love life! What is your business plan for love? If you are already married or partnered, look back to the person you were when you fell in love with your partner, or better, ask yourself how your partner embodies the traits you love right now. Often, we take these things for granted over time. Take a moment to write your own manifesto of your ideal relationship.

REFLECTION AND SOUL SEARCH

Why do you want a partner? (Really think about this. As with money, trying to fill a void is not the answer.)

_____

_____

_____

What are the top three health/physical characteristics you want in a partner? (You can brainstorm more and prioritize but be flexible on the rest because no one is perfect!)

_____

_____

_____

What are the top three emotional characteristics you want in a partner?

_____

_____

_____

Describe how this person deals with money and examine the similarities or differences in how you handle money.

_____

_____

_____

What are your thoughts on children, how many you want, and what roles you and your partner will each handle?

_____

_____

_____

Have you discussed how children will impact your finances, and how you will support your child's finances in education?

_____

_____

_____

How do you handle time constraints, like housework, meals, and other chores?

_____

_____

_____

What is your ideal home life and social life?

_____

_____

_____

What lifestyle goals do you wish to work toward with your partner?

_____

_____

_____

What work schedule would you each have, and what career choices would be attractive in an ideal partner?

_____

_____

_____

What work ethic should your partner have, and what should they accept from you?

_____

_____

_____

How will you motivate one another in your goals?

_____

_____

_____

Personally, I knew I needed another entrepreneur with a flexible schedule to help with parenting, and who would empathize with my unpredictable work schedule. I wanted someone who worked hard, but who also knew to take time off to play, and who treasured time with family.

My current husband helped his wife in raising his stepchildren. He was recently widowed when we met, but he had a bubbly, adorable personality. He is perhaps the kindest and sweetest person I have ever met. And I thought he was a big, sexy, manly man. Not too many men can wrap their arms around me because I'm a big, 6'1" lady. He had a successful business, but he was also passionate about golf and preparing great meals for his family. He loves my son. Life is still stressful, but I feel grounded. I have the resources to bring me back to center, with a partner who works by my side to build a life we agree on together. One of my biggest requirements was that my partner be very open to discussing money matters. As a former banker, himself, I found it refreshing to communicate so openly about our finances!

Chapter 11
Mary Beth Franklin,
the 2 A·M· Epiphany, and Passion

"Be open to the twists and turns in life."

— Mary Beth Franklin

WHEN I STARTED WRITING THIS book, I was still unclear about its focus, other than knowing I wanted to share my insights from several years as a financial advisor. Then Karen Putz asked me, "Who do you most admire whom you would like to interview?" Without a moment's hesitation, I said, "Mary Beth Franklin." Her quote on turning points had a formative influence on the direction this book would eventually take.

I met Mary Beth at an Investment News Conference a few years ago, only a few months after going independent as a wealth manager. A lot of talking heads were present, but Mary Beth came across as authentic, real, and not at all dry and boring, even though her subject of Social Security could be a potential yawner.

The conference itself was amazing. I met financial advisors from many different types of firms and walks of life. My mind was blown! I didn't know there were more flavors of financial advisors than ice cream at Baskin Robbins. I also noticed there weren't a lot of women. Even at the women's conference, many women were subordinate to men in wealth management groups; many were paraplanners, but few were independent advisors like me.

Mary Beth Franklin's regular articles in *Investment News* really changed my perspective on my responsibility to my clients in helping them plan when and how to take Social Security. Since that conference, I have even accompanied clients to the Social Security office to ask questions and help them file. I now have some great tools in my arsenal to examine Social Security strategies and look at what works best for each person or couple. It truly is an individual decision. There is no catch-all strategy that works best for everyone.

Besides public speaking and writing for *Investment News*, Mary Beth Franklin serves on the WIN Council. She also advises the CFP (Certified Financial Planner) Board and assists with initiatives to increase the number of women entering the financial planning profession.

I was terrified to email Mary Beth Franklin. Here was a prominent woman in the industry, and who was I? I was just another financial advisor in the sea of financial advisors with whom she had spoken. But having just read Karen Putz's book *Unwrapping Your Passion*, I was on a high that would not be shut down. And it was the holidays, so yes, maybe I had taste-tested one too many of the cookies I had baked that Sunday morning.

So I popped off an email to *the* Mary Beth Franklin, a gushing email about how awesome I thought it was that she had earned her CFP in her early sixties, something I have been struggling to do since forty-five, while juggling my career, motherhood, a recent second marriage, and humanitarian work.

Less than two hours later, she emailed me: "Thanks, Jody. I would be delighted to chat with you. I just turned sixty-four yesterday, so it seems like a timely conversation."

When I told Karen, my co-author, "Oh, my gosh! Mary Beth Franklin [blah blah blah]. I'm freaking out. In a good way," she enthusiastically replied, "Yessssssss" with eight ss.

My mind raced as I impatiently waited several days for the conference call.

The rest of this chapter recaps some of what we talked about that day.

Mary Beth Franklin became renowned more than thirty years ago working in the "eat what you kill" newspaper industry as a Capitol Hill reporter for United Press International, covering Washington, DC politics. Like many '80s ladies, she worked, married, and had children by her thirties. She didn't give up her career when she had children.

She embodied the Enjoli perfume commercial from the 1980s with Peggy Lee singing "I'm a Woman." In a tight business suit dress, with whips flowing blond hair, and a frying pan—she was the kind of woman who did it all and took no prisoners.

Mary Beth Franklin was so open and authentic, sharing with me her 2 a.m. epiphany. She explained how life has its twists and turns, and though we may feel very strong in our Money Messages, life paths, and wealth's purpose, sometimes the dream shifts—and it's okay to adjust the sails!

For Mary Beth, that shift happened at 2 a.m. If you can imagine, after commuting, working incredible hours at her successful journalist job, and doing all the "mom" stuff in the evening, Mary Beth finally got to rest her head on a pillow. Then her infant woke up crying at 2 a.m., her dog got sick on the floor, and her other child, a toddler, woke up. She was exhausted, and still had to go to work the next day.

She knew something had to change. Fortunately, she was open to the twists and turns in life. Today, she tells people to listen to that whisper when it tells you, "Maybe I should do something different," regardless of your age. Mary Beth realized she needed to work from home. She couldn't keep commuting to DC.

Mary Beth had written a few articles on politics and retirement benefits, so she had discovered a niche in the retirement world, with people clamoring for more knowledge about retirement planning and senior issues.

This 2 a.m. epiphany led her to become a syndicated columnist at Maturity News Service/Third Age Media, where she was able to work from home. Later, her writings on retirement led her to an amazing, thirteen-year career, with Kiplinger.

While working at Kiplinger, she had a conversation with her siblings. She was the youngest of five kids, so her siblings were already claiming Social Security. They were complaining about how they had to give most of it back to the government because they were still working. Mary Beth replied, "That's stupid. Let me look into it." As a result of this research, on July 1, 2008, Mary Beth published "Secret Ways to Boost Your Social Security," which became a popular article for *Kiplinger's Magazine*.

The result? Bags and bags of mail...the kind of mail Santa gets at Christmas. She had hit on an important heartstring for her audience; they had an enormous appetite for Social Security information. Mary Beth would spend nearly an hour every morning sorting through the mail and answering questions for her readers. She became known as the "Social Security expert" and was invited to speak at more and more events.

Then the whisper came again. She became passionate about public speaking but was limited by her employer. *Kiplinger's*, as one of the most ethical financial publications of the time, would not allow her to be compensated for outside business activities, including public speaking. So, the time, travel, and energy required to pursue this passion was on her dime, and it put her behind on the work she *did* get paid for.

On a chance encounter, *Investment News* approached Mary Beth to speak. She declined, saying she wasn't allowed to be compensated for her efforts, and it just didn't make sense for her financially. The event organizer then asked, "What would it take to get you to speak at our event and come work with us?"

After considering her options, Mary Beth decided to shift in her path. It was one of those moments that my co-author Karen Putz calls "synchronicity."

If you know where your passion lies, you can hear the whisper of opportunity when it calls. And opportunity was calling Mary Beth. She negotiated what she needed for her income and work flexibility to allow herself to focus more on travel and speaking and still be able to write. She negotiated for her future and her passion.

Life is too short to miss opportunities to pursue your passions! You are worth it, and it's always nice to be compensated for working at what you love. As Mary Beth Franklin says, "Be open to the twists and turns in life."

Here are a few questions to prepare you for learning how to Flip Your Script in the next chapter.

REFLECTION AND SOUL SEARCH

Where in my life do I feel crabby, overwhelmed, anxious, or stressed? What causes these emotions?

_____

_____

_____

Where do I feel these emotions in my body: my head, my chest, shoulders, sinuses, legs, back?

_____

_____

_____

How can I interpret these emotions? For instance, is this feeling temporary or long term? Is the feeling due to something physical like lack of sleep, or is it due to a situation that needs to be addressed?

_____

_____

_____

What would help me feel better, and switch these emotions to excitement, anticipation, and joy?

_____

_____

_____

What is the vision of what I would like my life to be?

_____

_____

_____

Do I look at work as a burden or a pleasure?

_____

_____

_____

How can I get the compensation I need in a job I love?

_____

_____

_____

Do I need to move on, or not?

_____

_____

_____

How do I make a plan, so I don't just quit when I'm fed up, with no way to support myself and move forward effectively?

_____

_____

_____

Is there a way to negotiate with my employer or my loved ones, or change something in myself, to make my work and life more enjoyable?

_____

_____

_____

Mary Beth made an amazing point in our interview about one of the biggest challenges some retirees face. They are escaping *from* their jobs, instead of escaping *to* a new phase in their lives: retirement.

One of the places Mary Beth is now invited to speak is The Villages north of Orlando. When you visit The Village's website (www. thevillages.com), you are greeted with active seniors playing water polo, dancing, and holding hands with a handsome, mature partner, walking into the sunset. It's a vision for the generation that loves the "Disney" lifestyle, the luxury-inclusive experience-at-your-fingertips lifestyle. Mary Beth, however, mentioned that everyone's ideal retirement vision and dream differs. While many people dream of margaritas and a beach, Mary Beth would not enjoy that lifestyle in retirement; she loves the bustle of the East Coast metropolitan areas, hopping on a subway to see a cultural or political event.

One challenge Mary Beth often finds her retired readership facing is they have a fantasy of the perfect retirement and wait and save for that "someday," only to be disappointed when it arrives. For example, imagine the retiree who is so excited about traveling the country in an RV in retirement, only to discover he doesn't really like to travel or drive the RV.... Or the retiree who worked so hard to accumulate monetary wealth but isn't emotionally able to spend it in the distribution phase, the retirement time, of her life. Sometimes, people don't plan out the phases of retirement, which can last decades. Mary Beth colorfully described it as the "Go go, slow go, no go" phases of retirement.

Regardless of your phase of life, be prepared to face the 2 a.m. epiphany. Check in with your passion and your perceptions of your situation. Be open to the many turning points you will face, even later in life, and learn how to effectively Flip the Script.

Chapter 12
Flip the Script

"So much has been given to me. I have no time to ponder that which has been denied."

— Helen Keller

M Y GRANDFATHER WAS BLIND, AND he always showed me possibilities. He was mischievous and stubborn, and if someone told him it was impossible for him to do something, especially because he was blind, he would overcome any obstacle, just to prove a point.

Some Money Messages limit. Some Money Messages open the universe.

The Money Messages you choose to have running through your head all day will also run through your life. When you have negative Money Messages, or you face turning points as your life moves forward, or you evolve as a person, you will need to "Flip the Script" to change the flow of energy around your emotions and your money.

In *The Atlantic*, I recently read Joe Pinsker's article, "People Are Confused About the Usefulness of Buying Fancy Things: Why luxury goods don't impress, but repel."[1]

---

1   https://getpocket.com/explore/item/people-are-confused-about-the-usefulness-of-buying-fancy-things?utm_source=pocket-newtab. Accessed December 16, 2019.

Pinsker quotes a couple of studies that validate some of *my own* hypotheses:

- The opposite of gratitude is wanting.

- The opposite of peace and happiness is dissatisfaction and depression.

- What you believe others think about you may not be true and, more importantly, is irrelevant to your own goals.

- There are always three ways to look at a situation: what we think is happening (the money story we tell ourselves), what is actually happening (the reality of the situation), and how we can adjust our thinking to our benefit (positive Money Messages).

One study Pinsker mentions describes a phenomenon of guilt over luxury purchases; we will look for an excuse or justification for the purchase, which he terms a "functional alibi." One excuse we use is that it will make us friends, but it seems the opposite is true.

Another study states:

> When making new friends, people tend to think that displaying high-status markers of themselves (e.g., a BMW, a Tag Heuer watch) will make them more attractive to others than neutral markers (e.g., a Honda, a generic brand watch); however, from the perspective of would-be friends, individuals who display high-status markers are found to be less attractive as new friends than those with neutral status markers.

I would highly recommend reading the full Pinsker article and the two studies.

Bottom line: Why should other people's real or imagined perceptions influence our spending? What we need to change is our *own* perceptions. We need to check into the reality of where our thoughts are coming from, not what we believe society or other people think about us! I hope that by releasing others' real or imagined perceptions of how you live your life, you feel freer. If you want to change your world, the real power you hold is *your ability to change your thoughts*. And here's another goal to consider: What steps can you take to make your situation better, without over-leveraging debt?

Look at the Money Messages below. I've listed those I gathered through research in one of my women's networks, and then I examined and elicited feedback on how we can make these messages more positive. Which of these Money Messages do you tell yourself? Can you see how you can flip the script just by looking at the same situation in a different way? Are there other Money Messages where you can flip the script for yourself?

REFLECTION AND SOUL SEARCH

Negative Money Messages	Positive Money Messages
I have bad Money Messages I learned when I was little.	I can find positive lessons on how to live my life, even if my environment had negative messages or influence when I was little.
I am in a worse financial position than my parents.	My parents' financial position has no bearing on how I view my life and my success.
I only seem to make bad money choices.	I can make better money choices, one day at a time.
I feel out of control when it comes to dealing with money.	I have control, through shifting my mindset and choices, over my financial situation.
I avoid thinking about money and how it affects my life.	Money is a tool for my lifestyle, and I no longer need to be scared.

I worry about money a lot.	I am making plans to move physically or emotionally to a space where I will worry less about money.
I feel lost when it comes to thinking about my future wealth.	I am making steps and plans for my current and future wealth.
When others speak of money, I feel triggered or angry.	When others speak of money, I feel indifferent or curious.
When life throws a curveball, I cave in or feel overwhelmed.	When life throws a curveball, I figure out my next steps.
I feel a sense of lack or scarcity.	I am grateful for what I have.
Friends or family criticize what I have (or don't have).	I will tap into those family members, friends, and resources that support my growth. I will surround myself with positive money and life messages.
Money is for selfish people./ Money is the root of all evil.	Money is simply an exchange of energy that can be used for self-care and helping others.
Being able to improve my situation is hopeless.	I am hopeful about my prospects for the future.
I'm not worth it.	I deserve to be fairly compensated.
I can't change anything.	I can make my financial situation better.
I'm stuck financially.	I can make small and big steps to move forward each day.

I procrastinate on saving.	I will pay myself first.
I binge-spend when I'm unhappy.	When I'm unhappy, I work to identify why, and look for healthy ways to fill the void besides spending.
My partner and I don't talk about money.	My partner is an important person in financial decisions.
I closely tie my emotions to how much money I have.	The amount of money I have doesn't affect my feelings of self-worth.

Now that you get the idea, take time to write down all the negative Money Messages that live in your head. Then flip the script by writing down a new, positive version of each message.

Practice Flipping Your Script	

When Life Throws a Twist

Chuck Poulin understands better than most how life can throw you for a twist. Having survived the housing market collapse in 2007, and continuing to work in the mortgage industry, he admits he has struggled with his own Money Messages. He's always felt that if you work hard, you will be successful, but even today, as an executive-level area manager in the mortgage industry, Chuck admits he can get stressed. "Sometimes, when I stress about money, I'll take a step back. I'll go to church and look at what's most important in my life. It's not bad. Tomorrow's another day, and as long as you have a brain, you can make money."

In 2014, Chuck experienced a major bump in his life: cancer. That experience also changed how he thought about money:

> In 2014, I'm having chemo pumped in my body, my daughter was five, my son was three, my wife was a stay-at-home mom. I could have given up. I could have caved in. I don't look at things the same way. Enjoy what you do. You'll always be good at living within your means if you stay happy. You should have a plan and save for the future but live in the present.

Rather than think about money as just a means to retire, Chuck also focuses on enjoying the now:

> It's something for me that I don't know if I will ever retire. Every day I'm very blessed that no matter my age, I can work in this career. When I get older, I may not do it at the high level I'm doing it now, but I could do this up until I'm sixty-five or seventy. I didn't have my daughter until I was thirty-nine and my son at forty-one, so I'm going to be in my sixties when they're in their twenties.
>
> And that's the "balance thing." People look at themselves and ask, "What do I need? What do we need to be happy—the

biggest house on the block with the biggest yard?" It's not the nicest car, the nicest school; it is not having anything. You know what it is for me? It's having a kid who's adjusted, who can adjust, who is confident, and who works hard. I have a relationship with my son and daughter. I can talk to them and watch them grow up. I can smile and be there for their successes, their failures, and help them and be part of their lives. To me, that is more important than money.

Although the cancer will never go away, it's not spreading and it's dormant. I'm very well on my way to being cancer-free in a few years. And I was stage four!

My outlook on life has changed. I still work hard, but I enjoy the hustle more. I love helping people get mortgages that change their lives and make their dreams come true. But if I want to take a day off to go golfing, I just do it. I don't know what the future holds because of what happened with my cancer. Retirement means you get to do what you want to do, when you want to do it. And I love what I do now, so I guess I'm always in retirement! As long as I enjoy what I do, I'll continue to do it. That makes sense…. I'm going to enjoy life now, when I'm healthy, because I've had my health taken away, and I got it back.

We all have ups and downs. Hopefully, you will not have to deal with cancer, a demanding career, and small children all at the same time, but life can throw some big curveballs. When the negative Money Messages are floating around in your head, stay focused on your dreams. Stay focused on those one or two visions in your life, whether it's the smile of your children, your religious faith, a walk on the beach, or helping at a homeless shelter that gives your life purpose. Then put that purpose behind your decisions about money. Check in with your list of negative Money Messages from time to time and keep a list of positive Money Messages close at hand. Whether you use a journal or sticky notes, your phone or your computer, keep your messages handy when you feel overwhelmed. Identify what messages you are telling yourself, and how you can flip them to make your emotions and your money situation better. Flipping the script takes daily practice. That doesn't mean you can get rid of negative Money Messages overnight and that they will go away forever, or that once it happens, it will always be solid. This is a daily practice. Flipping the script is a continual practice in your life.

Your beliefs become your thoughts,
Your thoughts become your words,
Your words become your actions,
Your actions become your habits,
Your habits become your values,
Your values become your destiny.

— Mohandas Karamchand Gandhi

PART III
INVESTING IN YOU

Chapter 13
Money Messages and
Your Investing Behavior

"The stock market is a wonderfully efficient mechanism for transferring wealth from the impatient to the patient."

— Warren Buffett

THROUGH CONTINUING EDUCATION AND IN my own observations, I have witnessed various archetypes, behaviors, and biases in investing. Some are consistent. Some appear from time to time in people, depending on what life situations and stresses pop up. Some are ingrained, part of the internalized Money Messages inherited or experienced over time.

The trick is to use positive Money Messages to reduce the emotional biases that hold you back from success. It is unrealistic to say you can eliminate these archetypes, behaviors, and biases. Even the best financial advisors let their biases creep in. We are human, too, so we financial advisors need clear processes to guide us in helping our clients.

I start out each review with a client by reiterating the pitfalls in investor behavior, and how I and the client can try to avoid it.

Industry research has shown that investors often make poor decisions that contribute to underperformance, including:

- Allowing emotion to guide investment decisions.

- Abandoning a long-term approach to chase last year's winners.

- Buying relatively overvalued investments while ignoring relatively undervalued investments.

- Losing patience during a period of volatility and pulling out of the market or trying to time the market.

"You shouldn't spend much time on your investments. That will just tempt you to pull up your plants and see how the roots are doing, and that's very bad for the roots.
It's also very bad for your sleep."

— Paul Samuelson,
Winner of the Nobel Memorial Prize in
Economic Sciences

Loss Aversion

Do you know someone who squirrels away cash, or money in savings, and never invests it? Or worse, just spends it, saying, "Carpe diem," because if you don't spend it, the government, taxes, death, surprise catastrophes, or insert whatever excuse you want, is just going to make it disappear, and you'll never enjoy it?

Loss aversion is where I see people become the most irrational. Many are holding onto a huge Money Message of LACK in capital letters. If you put aside money for fun and emergencies, the lack will disappear, leaving you *more* money to invest and grow. It is amazing how one little mindset shift coupled with purposeful action will change your life.

I do think emergency savings (not invested) of at least six months is valuable, but after that, the money should be invested for the future, or more immediate plans should be made for your lifestyle goals. Yes, you can lose money investing in the stock market or in property. But think about this: If cash is sitting in your drawer, your house could burn down, or a burglar (or your teenager) could take it. Yes, risk exists no matter what you do. If you don't invest money somehow, you will be losing money to inflation, or to status spending, or spending on false promises. *You* are the real promise. Invest in you. Pay yourself first. You are worth it. Make the changes in your Money Messages, and your life, today.

Investing Archetypes

Most of the following archetypes appear before me when someone has become obsessed with winning or losing money. It manifests itself through extreme worry. This worry is usually rooted in a person's history, their Money Messages.

See what archetypes you can identify in yourself, and how you might identify these behaviors and how they can limit your success in investing.

REFLECTION AND SOUL SEARCH

Put a checkmark in the box, if you think you sometimes feel like this:

Investor Archetypes

- ❑ **The Gambler**: This person is obsessed with winning the big one. He or she truly believes winning the lottery is just a matter of time. Putting money on a losing bet, or a penny stock, with the thought of being the one in a million makes sense to the gambler. Instead of taking the slow road, or the path of patience, this person will repeatedly make bets with the money in hopes of being the winner. Often, this person jumps from one financial advisor to another, looking for the one with the "secret sauce." As losses compound, the person's behavior becomes more erratic. Inevitably, the gambler will always be disappointed and blame their failure on others, instead of looking inward at what a mess all the jumping around and gambling bets has caused, or worse, the gambler will walk away from the table completely, telling themselves they are better living with the losses than staying in the game. (See also The Ostrich).

- ❑ **The Skydiver:** Much like the Gambler, the Skydiver is a risk taker who will take large sums of money and put them at great risk to win. However, this risk taker is more calculated than the Gambler. Instead of putting money in the lottery, this person is more likely to place the bets in day trading or do "research" to try to beat the market. As a newer skydiver, she will check and recheck the jump pack before getting on the plane, and she is ready and able to jump into the open air. However, if she's only learned how to pack a parachute by watching a YouTube video, how effective will she be when she jumps? Does she have a jump instructor with her, or is she smarter than the jump instructor who has done thousands of jumps, because she read about skydiving on the internet? Or better, she got a lot of great advice from her cousin, or perhaps her mechanic, who has been parachuting about six times a year for the past five years and has it all figured out.

❑ **The Existentialist:** This person is fatalistic about investing and the market. "I'm probably going to lose money in the market, so I might as well just enjoy today and not save. I should save short-term and use it all on vacations, because by 'retirement age' I'll be too old to enjoy it." While it's tempting to embrace "carpe diem," I would encourage you to save for both short-term and long-term goals, at the same time. We will discuss this later when we get to Chapter 14 Buckets: Paying Off Debt. You may not get the immediate gratification if you save half for long term, and put half in a vacation savings account, but at least you will have something for emergencies, for now, and for further down the road. There is nothing sadder to me, than when I see a person struggling by on Social Security because nothing was saved when he or she was younger. Social Security was only meant to supplement your retirement at 25-30 percent of what you made during your career. Could you live on 30 percent of your current paycheck? If you can't do it now, how will you do it later? Would it be easier to learn to live on 80 or 90 percent of what you make now, and save the rest?

❑ **The Ostrich:** This person invests, but only in things that are "safe." This is the kind of person you would see at the bank getting a toaster (when they still gave out toasters) for opening an IRA CD (Individual Retirement Account Certificate of Deposit). I still occasionally meet elderly people, the Depression-era Greatest Generation, who say, "Oh, yes, I have several IRAs." What they really mean is, "I have opened several IRA CDs at different banks." They have them because they think those CDs will give them better performance and diversification. If I may share a dirty little secret, CDs, while FDIC insured, only give you the lowest possible interest rate you are willing to tolerate, in exchange for a government guarantee of principal and interest at maturity, regardless of the bank you are investing in. The bank turns around and lends your money at higher rates to businesses and people getting mortgages, and for paying their overhead. While CDs provide a great place to park some of your emergency money, if you take no risk with the majority of your money, you will lose money to inflation. Inflation usually ticks ahead of CD rates by .25 to .5 percent.

❑ **The Wandering Farmer:** Have you ever heard the saying, "Don't put all your eggs in one basket?" Some misguided people believe this means they should have their money at several different institutions. They may have smaller amounts of money at two or three brokerage firms, maybe five or six different banks. I have no problem with a client, particularly if they have a sizeable portfolio, using one or two banks, and perhaps two different financial advisors. It's sad to say, but the person with the biggest basket of eggs usually gets better pricing. You will often pay higher management fees or commissions, or you will get lower interest rates on CDs, if you are investing a smaller amount for a shorter time. It's also important that all your advisors know what each other is doing, and that they are not being "pitted" against one another. I would look at them as providing complementary services. Perhaps one advisor can find you amazing rates on bonds while your other advisor focuses on good managed accounts. Perhaps one bank provides great CD rates, while your other bank has great benefits for checking accounts. If you are not strategic in *why* you are using different advisors, you are *not* putting your eggs in different baskets; you are putting your baskets on different farms. If your strategy is the same with each financial advisor, chances are, the portfolios may use different securities, but you are duplicating efforts. That is not diversification. That is just wandering.

Biases

Which of the following biases are you susceptible to? Check any that apply to you.[2]

☐ **Anchoring or Confirmation Bias:** Over-reliance on what one thinks rather than looking at actual data.

☐ **Regret Aversion or Loss Aversion:** Wanting to avoid the feeling of regret experienced after making a choice with a negative outcome. This aversion can cause an investor to be reluctant to sell losing investments.

☐ **Disposition Effect:** Labeling individual investments as winners or losers. While some investments can cause loss, looking at short-term performance in a funnel is also dangerous.

☐ **Hindsight:** After the fact, believing the onset of past events was predictable and completely obvious, when, in fact, the event could not have been reasonably predicted.

☐ **Familiarity Bias:** The tendency to stick with what is known and having anxiety when diversifying to lesser known investments.

☐ **Self-Attribution Bias:** Attributing successful outcomes to one's own actions and blaming bad outcomes on external factors.

☐ **Trend-Chasing Bias:** Chasing past performance in the mistaken belief that historical returns predict future performance.

☐ **Worry:** Though the act of worrying is natural, it evokes memories and creates visions of possible future scenarios that alter an investor's objective judgment on investments.

---

2   This list is adapted from coursework from the College for Financial Planning.

With human emotion, how can we possibly become successful at investing? It looks like we humans may be emotional freak shows if you read all the archetypes and biases above. Please understand, I am not being facetious as I write this chapter. I personally have suffered from nearly all the above afflictions at one point or another in my own investing. I have a particular affinity to the skydiver, myself, but only with my own money, and only with a small amount. It must be money I am willing to lose completely. I will guide my fellow skydivers in the same approach, if they really want that hot shiny stock out there. But for the rest of us who can't afford to gamble or skydive, I recommend discipline, patience, time, and an allocation consistent with your goals and an ability to handle the ups and downs of the market. I know you may be giving me a big eye roll right now, given that I am a financial advisor, but I strongly recommend you hire an advisor, someone who's at least five years in the business, and interview them to find the right fit for you. I have other advisors I consult with all the time for my clients and my own investments. Just as a good therapist uses a therapist (and who in our society couldn't use a good therapist?) a good financial advisor is not a lone ranger, so why would you be? For help in finding the right advisor, check out "How to Find a Financial Advisor" in the Bonus Section.

Chapter 14
Buckets: Paying Off Debt

"I don't want money to make my life decisions for me. I had to figure out a way to live the way I wanted with the money I have. Learn to live without the things you can't have. Take the competition out of your living and learn the difference between wants and needs."

— Ann, Client

Now it's time for one of the most important lessons in this book:

Buckets.

If you have debt, you must pay it off. Period.

But how?

Buckets that you fill up, buckets that you take from. Some people might call this a gas tank, a reserve, a fund, or the dreaded work "budget." I hate the word "budget." A bucket is simply how we divide up the money we have, the money coming in, and the money we have going out.

I invite you now to get a piece of paper and compartmentalize your buckets by broad categories (net income, fixed expenses, and variable expenses) or complete the forms provided below. Then if you know how to use a spreadsheet, you can narrow down your buckets into sub-categories such as household and business (and children if you wish). I would prefer you keep it very simple at this point. I think sometimes we can overcomplicate a task, and then we end up procrastinating and never diving in.

REFLECTION AND SOUL SEARCH

NET INCOME:

(Net Income is the income you receive from your paycheck after taxes)

Source	Amount

Total Net Income: $_____

FIXED EXPENSES:

(These would be an average of your utilities, mortgage or rent, insurance payments, retirement savings, monthly subscriptions, credit card payments)

Fixed Expense	Amount

Total Fixed Expenses: $_____

VARIABLE EXPENSES:

(These would be going to restaurants, clothing, groceries, etc.)

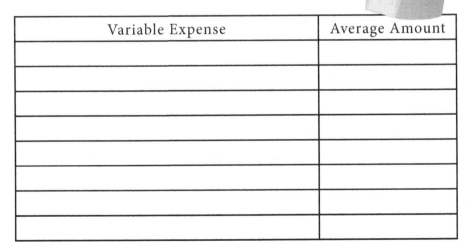

Variable Expense	Average Amount

Total Variable Expenses: $_____

If your income is less than your expenses, which expenses can be cut or reduced? If you can't cut or reduce anything, can you do something to earn more money? Sometimes solutions to having more than you spend are small, sometimes drastic. It may come down to soul searching about where you live, whether better career opportunities exist in another town, or cutting some high-cost discretionary expenses until you can get your budget back on track and pay off your debt. Bottom line: You must have more coming in than going out.

If you don't have more money coming in than going out, you either need to:

A. Make more money.

B. Find a way to spend less.

The most important goal is intention. Assigning purpose to your money allows you to understand your spending and priorities.

Here is a little more detail on intention. In this second step, we will sort our buckets based on needs or wants. Needs and wants can be debatable, and sometimes, they will hit your triggers and tap into those negative Money Messages. If this is happening for you right now, I encourage you to *breathe* and adjust your mindset to indifference and curiosity.

REFLECTION AND SOUL SEARCH

In this exercise, I'd like you to take the income or expenses that filled your buckets, and now list them in a different way. Determine whether the expense is a need or a want on the left, and on the right, I would like you to brainstorm ideas on how you could change (or not change) that expense to your advantage. I put a few items in as examples for you to see, and then you try!

INCOME/ EXPENSE	COST (Month)	NEED/ WANT	IDEA	REVISED COST
Rent	$700	N	Rent (Room-mate)	$350
Car lease	$650	N	No change, stuck in lease 3 years	$650
Magazine Subscription	$35	W	Cut out, not reading it	$0
Nanny	$3,064	W	Daycare	$1,150
TOTAL	**$4,449**		TOTAL	$2,150

Now you try, using your income, fixed expenses, and variable expenses!

INCOME/ EXPENSE	COST (Month)	NEED/ WANT	IDEA	REVISED COST
TOTAL				

You may quickly identify things that shouldn't be in your buckets at all anymore. They might be monthly subscriptions you don't use, or expenses you determine are no longer necessary, like a gym membership, a magazine you never read, or that professional service you never use. Set aside time to weed these things from your financial garden. You may want to remove these items from your buckets. Write a new list on a separate piece of paper and tick off the list over the next few days to cut these items. This exercise is very liberating, so I try to do it once or twice a year. I imagine you will magically find $100 or more just with this simple exercise. I do!

I would also recommend paying fixed expenses from one checking account, and that you fill the account with at least two to six months of total balance needed for those expenses. Review it each month and refill it. Keep an eye out for changes in your bills, which will mean you will need to adjust your "fill the bucket" total next month. I pay nearly all my fixed expenses by auto-debit, shortly after my income deposit, so it takes no thought or stress. Paying the fixed bills just happens…before I spend it on other things.

Pay variable expenses from a different checking account and give yourself an allowance so you can't spend more than that.

I use different banks for different types of personal and business expenses, and further divide them by fixed and variable expenses. Each of these accounts has a "cushion" of two to six months for each category. I am a visual person, so each of my cards is a distinct and different color. I also have a savings account where I put money not in my monthly "allowance" and keep it in a bucket (figuratively speaking) as my emergency money.

In addition, my savings for retirement and education are set up like bills, auto-debited from the fixed account into their respective investment accounts. When I had credit card debt, and successfully paid it off, I stopped—I repeat *stopped*—using credit cards. I paid the old debt like a utility bill and made more than the minimum payment. Everything else was on a cash basis.

I am happy to say that by using this simple strategy, I have stayed debt free since paying it off four years ago, and my husband and I will have our mortgage paid off within the next three years.

I don't pour over my bills. I just increased my savings more recently. We eat out a few times a month, I go on vacations (albeit modest ones), and I splurge on garden supplies. I want for nothing, and I am happier than I ever was.

Are there moments of worry? Sure. I'm human. But I feel much more in control because I set up a game plan and I stick to it.

Chapter 15
Creating Your Plan B

*"The most successful people are the ones who are good
at Plan B. Only through trials and failures we can learn
what works and what doesn't, and this brings the needed
knowledge that we need to understand why it's not
working."*

— James A. Yorke, Distinguished Research Professor of
Mathematics and Physics,
University of Maryland, College Park

S O MANY LIFE COACHES AND motivational videos preach against
"Plan B."

Linda Conroy, the herbal conferences organizer I mentioned back
in Part I, lives from the land, and often turns to barter/trade over
traditional money systems. She trusts that her resources and basic
needs will always be taken care of, but that doesn't mean she doesn't
prepare. When I interviewed her, she told me:

> I don't need to have a lot of money, but it's important to me
> that I know what I have as an entrepreneur. I know things wax
> and wane. I've been an entrepreneur for gosh, twenty years
> now. Most of my adult life I've supported myself with my own

business, so I've gotten used to that anxiety. I have heeded the advice that it's a good idea to have at least six months, to be able to pay your rent for six months, just to make sure you have your needs covered. In that way, in case there's a transition, or a need for a different decision, you can do something different and shift gears. I think to myself, *Okay, if my business starts to wane, I always have a Plan B.*

Figuring out Plan B before it's needed isn't going to eliminate all anxiety, but it can provide support in pursuing a different path when life happens.

When things do wax and wane, Linda has other tools in her kit. She becomes more active, and she finds ways to connect with other people. She isn't afraid to invite support from her network, whether it's reaching out to invite people to her classes or drumming up business in the products she sells. "I remind myself, 'Okay, you have been able to do this; you've been able to get through different transitions in the past years.'"

Linda continued, "I personally have had a lot of transition in my life, and it's been interesting to see that my business has such a nice foundation that even through my personal transition and sometimes feeling anxious, it's taking care of itself." She will also reach out to close friends to help bring her emotional frequency higher when she needs reassurance. If you've ever met Linda, you know she is a *force.*

Below are some ideas and exercises to help you ride through transitions.

REFLECTION AND SOUL SEARCH

How to Ride Through Transitions:

1. Create a "Plan B"

In what areas of your life might you need to consider creating a Plan B, like a possible layoff, a slow time in your earnings, going from a two-spouse income to a one-spouse income, care of elderly parents, or another unexpected expense? *Example: My company has been downsizing, and I'm really worried I might get laid off.*

_____

_____

_____

_____

_____

2. Take Action

What ideas do you have to deal with these possible challenges? What steps can you take now, in advance, to address these possible challenges? *Example: I can't control getting laid off, but I can set up at least six months for expenses, and I can start a soft search for a more stable company.*

_____

_____

_____

3. Connect with Others

Who, or what organizations, can possibly assist you if you face a challenge? *Example: I am going to start attending evening networking events to meet more people in my industry and create professional friendships and networks outside my company.*

_____

_____

_____

4. Seek Support

What actions can you take now to connect with a support system if you face a challenge? *Example: I am going to seek out a headhunter to keep an eye out for me, and that way, I can keep my search more anonymous than posting my resume on a job search site.*

_____

_____

_____

5. Keep Your Focus

What self-care steps can you take to stay focused? *Example: In the meantime, I am going to go to the gym to keep my energy level high, and I'm going to set my intention to get seven hours of sleep a night. I think I need to talk to a doctor about my insomnia because I know getting good sleep is important for keeping my energy level high.*

_____

_____

_____

The idea of a Plan B is to use risk management to hopefully alleviate or eliminate catastrophic results. I believe risk management is essential, even as we pursue Plan A. Financial advisors, insurance agents, and even the space program make use of risk management to create the safest experience in a risky environment, to hopefully have the best outcomes.

If we were not to consider Plan B—risk management—there would be no insurance industry. For most of us, car insurance, health insurance, and renters or homeowners' insurance is important. Sure, you can drive a car without insurance, saying, "Oh, I'll never get in an accident!" The financial fallout if you did get in a car accident, particularly if you are at fault, however, would be devastating. And without proper health insurance, a car accident where you are hurt could be financially, and possibly physically, devastating.

In my previous life, I was certified in Project and Program Management by the University of Santa Cruz. I was taught by some of the most amazing teachers, including two instructors who helped in project and program management in the construction of the first space station for NASA. I heard some pretty funny stories in which, even when people thought they had considered all risks, the unexpected happened. One funny example is when they were testing a GPS tracker on a dolphin but forgot to tell the project team the tracker needed to be waterproof.

Nonetheless, we can still do our best to mitigate risks as we grow our wealth and maintain a positive mindset.

Plan B is also important in retirement. In the past, retirement was the point where you were no longer able to work, and so, you "retired." In the past, many people had pensions, but few people today still have the gift of a pension. Social Security covers a fraction of most people's lifestyle needs. And further, people are living longer. Plan B is not just about saving for retirement, but about what you do when the unexpected happens in retirement. We'll discuss some of these considerations in the next chapter.

Chapter 16
The Golden Years: Or Are They?

*"Retirement is like a long vacation in Las Vegas. The goal
is to enjoy it the fullest, but not so fully that
you run out of money."*

— Jonathan Clements

EVEN WITH THE BEST LAID plans, something will happen. Ben
Neiburger, an accomplished elder care attorney I've had the
opportunity to meet, refers to this situation as, "The slow train wreck."
Maybe this will first happen with an aunt or uncle. Maybe it will be your
parents. Perhaps it will be you. Most certainly it will be you, at some
point.

We die. But before we die, some of us live, for a while. For some of us,
death will be a slow process. For some of us, it will be unexpected and
sudden. What plans have you made for this inevitability, and the wreck-
age it leaves behind for your family? Are you aware that in the blink of
an eye your life can and most probably will be turned upside down?
Can you roll with a sudden change in your way of life? Can your partner, children, or parents roll with the punches? Is there a better way?

Absolutely. Plan for end of life when you are in a positive space, your
core feels strong, your energy is high, and you are feeling good about
life.

Think about the following questions:

- How will your life be remembered and celebrated?
- Can you let go of "the plan" and embrace or create a new dream?
- How can you (or can you) ease your loved ones into a different space if changes need to happen?
- What is the legacy you will leave behind?

It is important to speak to a lawyer regarding the legal documents, such as a trust or will, living will, and financial and health directives. I will go into more detail shortly on what things to consider and discuss with your lawyer. From an emotional perspective, I really love *The Five Wishes*, a workbook that delves more into the emotional and spiritual aspects of legacy planning. You can purchase it at fivewishes.org.

In the end, how do you wish to be remembered? Are there certain songs you would like to share with your loved ones to comfort them? What last words would you wish to say to your friends? Do you want to be seen in a casket, buried, or cremated? Your social and spiritual gifts are what are most remembered and passed on through the generations. I remember only fragments about my farming grandmother, but I do remember her caramel rolls, her love of gardening, and I have the sheet music to an old hymn, "My God and I," that was played at her funeral. My mother shared the music with me when I was learning piano and told me the story of it being her mother's favorite song. I worked so hard to learn that song. Every time I play it on the piano, it helps me feel a little closer to that love from her, from my childhood. She passed away more than forty years ago, but the smell of caramel rolls, gardening, and singing that song still remind me of her.

Before my husband John's mother died, I had the opportunity to play the song for her. Though she was in the final stages of dementia, she still sang along and remembered the words. It was touching that I could communicate with her through music as the rest of the world dimmed in her mind.

Would you like your grandchildren to remember something of you? *The Five Wishes* is a nice guide to help. If you don't wish to purchase that, could you sit down and write a journal of what you love, and what memories or ideas you would like generations after you to remember of you? And then give it to someone to share at your remembrance?

The perfect time to think about planning for end of life is when life is good: after a fun wedding, when a baby has graced the world with its miracle of life, when someone you love has celebrated a special birthday or anniversary. These are the times you can celebrate life being well lived.

Planning for the unexpected is hard because it's unexpected! But when you have all that feel-good mojo after a wedding, it's a great time to open the conversation.

Example: Henry, wasn't our daughter Sheena's wedding great? Are there ways we can make life easier for the kids as we get older? I mean, do you remember what my cousin Lisa just went through with her dad, having to clean out Uncle George's house, having to go through probate, and then the cousins fighting over who got the farmhouse table from Gramma Jean? Do you think we should clean up some of our junk, and maybe earmark some of the nicer pieces, like the grandfather clock, to see if Sheena or Henry Jr. would want them if something happened to us? I mean, if neither of them wants it, maybe we could see if a cousin might want it? And we could review our estate planning documents, because we do have a more complicated situation now than we did thirty years ago, especially with Henry Jr.'s ex-wife and the grandkids.

Consider the alternative: A tragedy has happened. Your family is tormented as they make decisions for you, because you may be unable to make those decisions for yourself. They are unsure what you would have wanted. You are weak, perhaps unable to speak, and perhaps your decision-making is impaired due to diminished mental capacity. In times of illness, I find the affected person sometimes clings to stuff, grieving the life lost. If the family already knows what their loved one wants, the ill person can be reminded. If no one knows, a lot of potential exists for misunderstandings and family fights.

My husband John and I were first challenged with the "slow train wreck" with his mother-in-law, the stepmom of his late first wife. She had given him medical power of attorney, the ability to make medical decisions, and entrusted him with helping on some financial affairs, but she had not given him financial power of attorney. She began falling into dementia, and had increasing health issues, making her unable to take care of her five basic care needs, also known as "Activities of Daily Living" (ADLs).

These five basic needs, according to the US Department of Health and Human Services (longtermcare.acl.gov) are:

- Bathing
- Dressing
- Transferring (moving to and from a bed or a chair)
- Eating
- Caring for incontinence

Because she didn't have the financial power of attorney in place, my husband John wasn't able to make the financial decision for when it was time for her to go into assisted care. My husband needed to work through the court system to get a court-appointed guardian to manage those decisions. It took months, a lot of money, and a lot of sleepless nights for my husband. Unfortunately, because of her state's laws, it was the only thing he could do.

If there's no medical power of attorney or living will, there's also no guidance on revival. For example, if someone has dementia, but doesn't have a DNR (do-not-resuscitate order), that person could potentially be put on feeding tubes when there is little quality of life left.

By contrast, John's own mother had a DNR with comfort measures only. When she came to the end of her life, she went through a few weeks where she would eat, and then not eat. When she finally stopped eating for good, she was given pain medication because her organs had stopped working, but she was not hooked up to feeding tubes to try to bring her back. She died peacefully, with her husband by her side, with minimal medical equipment hooked up to her. No one had to make the painful decision to allow her to die. She made that decision when she was still of sound mind.

As an adult child, it can be frustrating when you want to help; perhaps you ask your loved ones to get financial and medical power of attorney, a living will for wishes on life-saving measures, and a will or trust, but they refuse to do so. As a loved one, it leaves such a feeling of powerlessness and grief when you don't know what to do.

Create an Estate Plan

During a podcast I did with attorney Sonia Coleman, she told me, "One of the challenges I face is motivating people to commence and finish their estate plans. Often, I think people do not want to face the reality of death. So, they procrastinate on one of the most important things they can provide for their families."

What is an estate plan?

Most estate plans consist of at least an inventory of your accounts and a review of the beneficiaries, a will or a trust, a medical power of attorney, a living will, and a financial power of attorney. If you spell out what you want, it's more likely your wishes will be honored.

If you have dealt with caring for a parent or sibling and they had good estate planning, it's more likely you will put an estate plan in place for yourself. To prepare, you'll want to consider the following items before you meet with your attorney.

REFLECTION AND SOUL SEARCH

Legacy Planning

Questions for yourself:
1. Whom do you want running the show if you are disabled or dead? Do you have a child, sibling, or friend you trust?

_____

_____

_____

2. Do you need a will or a trust? It's good to ask your attorney this question and have him or her help you determine what is best.

_____

_____

_____

3. If you are alive and on life support, what do you want your family to do or not do?

_____

_____

_____

4. What will happen to your social media if you die or are disabled? Ask your attorney if there are legal provisions in your estate planning documents for this. More and more, I'm seeing attorneys paying attention to this in legacy planning.

_____

_____

_____

Questions for your attorney:

1. How many years of experience do you have?

_____

_____

_____

2. What kinds of clients have you served, and can you share some of the stories of how estate planning helped?

_____

_____

_____

3. Do you have any worksheets or binders I'll be able to share with my family after the estate plan is complete?

_____

_____

_____

4. Would you happen to have a free copy of *The Five Wishes* or other resources to help me deal with the emotional side of my legacy planning?

_____

_____

_____

5. Can you provide a proposal of what you will prepare for me, and an approximate cost? (In my experience, attorneys who have a written pricing sheet are usually efficient and cost-effective. Most attorneys generally have an estimate they will give you, but they can't provide an exact cost because they can't determine how much you will need or what revisions may come up. If they refuse to give you any price range, run away.)

_____

_____

_____

Here are some additional things you should consider for your estate plan as you think about creating emotional and financial freedom for yourself and your loved ones as you become older:

- Hire an attorney with experience in estate plans: It doesn't matter if you are twenty or seventy, it's not too early to enlist a good attorney to discuss what an estate plan means for you. A good attorney will help you determine what you need and walk you through the details of each legal instrument.

- Review your estate plan every five years, or sooner if there are major life changes.

- Share your estate plan with your family. Let your family know where to find the documents, and possibly provide copies, just in case they can't find them later. I had one client tell me when she went to her mother's house (her mother had dementia), they found part of her estate plan where it was supposed to be, and the other part in the bottom of a laundry basket. It's easy to say, "That won't happen to me." But what if it does?

- Get rid of the clutter in your personal life because it will influence your financial life as well. You may be familiar with Marie Kondo and the concept "If it doesn't give me joy, get rid of it." Living with less clutter will help you feel more peace in your surroundings, and, in turn, may help you improve your Money Messages. Unfortunately, Americans tie their self-worth to what they own and how much stuff they have. When I lived in France, I found people generally lived in much smaller houses and on smaller property spaces. They like pretty things, but I noticed how much sparser, but more beautiful, those pretty things were. My host mom carefully chose everything in her house, from the hand-embroidered napkins to the simple, elegant, but functionally sparse furniture in her house. In Sweden, there is a term called "döstädning," or death cleaning. In her book *The Gentle Art of Swedish Death Cleaning*, Margareta Magnussen discusses how to "make life run more smoothly," and celebrate the simplicity necessary for a happy life. Though it sounds morbid, the book is freeing and uplifting. The last thing you want to do is leave a massive disaster for your family to sort through. Plus, after you look at each item and decide, "Is this necessary to my life and happiness?", you can decide if it is something that can be sold and enhance your finances. My son recently outgrew his bicycle. I could have let it collect dust in the back of the garage; instead, I put it up for sale on a yard sale website. Within hours, I had $50 in my hands, the father was thrilled for his son to have such a cool bike, and I was happy knowing the bicycle was going to a good home to be used for a few more years.

- Leave part of your legacy now. If you have a special item intended for your children, and you don't use it daily, why not give it away now, and create a memory to share? You could give the item as a birthday or Christmas gift, or you could have a special meal and present something to the members of your family you invite. It can be a celebration where you share memories about the item(s). I have spoken to people who have received something through a bequest from a deceased loved one, who have said, "It would have been nice if they'd shared this with me years ago, so I could have heard the story about this item," or "I wish I could have told them I didn't really want this." Particularly with money, I have sometimes heard, "I wish Mom and Dad would have enjoyed life more and used some of this money for themselves." Regarding gifting money, if you are seventy or older, work with your financial advisor on your retirement income outlook. If it appears all your financial needs are met, this may be an option for you, but you have to really look at your situation before doling out the cash, and factor in things like inflation, your withdrawal rate, expected returns on your money, and management of catastrophic risks like health care issues or a market downturn.

- Plan for living with diminished capacity. After age fifty, or when your kids move away, whichever comes first, start thinking about downsizing and accessibility. My favorite way to think about this discussion is to use the "ice cream" game. If you have a partner, discuss it together. I originally heard of this game from a wholesaler at a mutual fund company, and I think it's a great way to think about accessibility and your living environment.

"What if I broke my arm and my leg? How would I get an ice cream cone?"

Would I have a shuttle service I could call? How would I get down the stairs to get to this shuttle service? Is there someone who could help me if I was in a wheelchair? Could someone bring me an ice cream cone? With one hand, how would I hold the ice cream cone? Who would clean up any mess? Could I get to the washer and dryer and run it with one hand to clean my clothes after eating my ice cream cone?

Let's apply this to other areas of your living situation and the things you keep. Would I still need my table saw, which has been sitting in the garage for ten years collecting more dust bunnies than sawdust? Would I need someone to scrub my floors, if I am unable to? Will I still be able to prepare meals for my family when they come and visit, or should I start looking at passing the torch to my adult children? Will my children want, or be able, to take care of me if I am unable to care for myself?

Considering all these questions will help you retain as much of your independence as possible as you grow older, while preparing you financially to have help if you need it. Your golden years have a better chance of being golden when you plan, financially and in all areas of your life.

Chapter 17
Tying It All Together: What's Next?

"More than anything else, saving is about creating freedom."

— David Weliver

I can't end my book with death and downsizing. That would be way too depressing. In nearly all the financial plans I help clients create, I stress the importance of (reasonable) allocation for play, travel, or hobbies. Retirement should be more than just surviving and preparing for death. If you don't plan for what's next, and what will help you and your family, you either:

a) won't live the life you truly want

or

b) will live a semi-charmed life.

You don't want to continue to live in a fog, unconscious, until you hit a brick wall—because that will be when you realize what you thought important really wasn't.

The final story I'd like to share is that of Mike Barker, my friend's father. I had the chance to interview him about his unique perspective on life and retirement.

Mike describes himself as a blessed man. His life wasn't always pretty. Growing up, he was a child of the steel industry. Everyone in his area worked in some fashion at U.S. Steel, or in occupations that complemented the steel industry. First opened as the North Chicago Railway Mill company in 1882, the plant was nestled between the Calumet River and Lake Michigan.

According to ForgottenChicago.com, "The neighborhood that developed around the mill, South Chicago, was filled with immigrants of all types who came to the area for the well-paying jobs at the mill." It was the leader in the steel industry, but by the 1970s, the heyday was over.

On April 10, 1992, the plant was closed forever. Mike describes the tragedy, "A whole generation was to go somewhere that no longer existed." Sons and daughters of these hard-working immigrants expected to always have jobs at the plant, but it was gone. "They put all their eggs in one basket, but the world changes."

Mike was the oldest of nine kids. His father was a union bricklayer all his life. They never starved, and his mom stayed at home. His parents lived paycheck to paycheck. His lessons in life about money and lifestyle came early. He wanted to go to Catholic high school, but the only way he could afford it was to work himself. He worked paper routes to pay for school and his supplies. He tried college, but he was immature and spent too much time partying, so he left to make some money since he no longer had enough to afford school.

Mike went into construction, alongside his dad, and started making a good living. He got married, had kids, and by chance, ended up in a good career that had nothing to do with construction. Mike took a job with the Lyric Opera with Chicago and ended up becoming their head flyman.

When he started the job, Mike knew very little about investing, and neither did many of his coworkers. Charlie, a part-time union rep, cornered Mike before he went in the room to sign up for his benefits. He told Mike, "You're stupid if you don't sign up for the retirement plan. When you go in there, put in 10 percent and don't even think twice."

Mike was grateful for Charlie's advice. "It doesn't matter what you make, you will still spend it, and you need to pay yourself first. If all that money is building up, you will be able to walk away with a stack of money. The key in all of this is time. If you are in your fifties, your window is shorter."

Mike doesn't remember if he told his first wife how much he was saving. "She didn't really care for the nuts and bolts of it, as long as it got done," he recalled. "The paycheck didn't really change that much, so it wasn't noticeable. It truly was money we never missed." Unfortunately, meeting the nuts and bolts of the job and his family obligations meant that Mike spent very long hours at his job. He worked 80-100 hours a week. His first wife got tired of being alone all the time, so they divorced. Life twists and turns. "Life happens," Mike told me, "but it's how we pull ourselves up, and make our lives better, and the lives of our kids better."

Five or six years later, Mike met his second wife while working at the opera. He jokes, "She just wanted a free dinner and we wound up together." He said the relationship built slowly, but eventually, they blended families, raising four girls and a boy. Two of his daughters ended up in education. He said he's always been blessed to have work, and his modeling what it is to be a hard worker carried over to his kids. "I instilled that work ethic into my kids, and they are all doing well." Sometimes he felt his family didn't save enough, but he was always able to work and take care of his family. After thirty years at his demanding career, when his kids were all grown and the youngest one moved to college in Arizona, he decided to take the big step into the journey called "retirement." He and his wife moved to Arizona, too—a great place to retire from the cold Chicago winters.

Mike had a friend, Bobby Lou Walker, who passed away a few years ago. Bobby Lou was a stagehand for *The Oprah Winfrey Show*, and had a quick wit. Mike describes him as a "good-old boy from Tennessee." Working as stagehands, Mike and Bobby Lou had long periods of downtime when they could hang out and visit. One day, when they were talking about life, Bobby Lou warned him, "When we rest, we rest. If we stay engaged, we stay alive."

Those words came back to Mike during his first year in retirement. Mike hated being "retired." He couldn't imagine watching TV or golfing all day, so in 2017, in his seventies, he re-enrolled in college to become a teacher. He always had a dream of completing a college degree, a dream he'd abandoned for many years. Though he had loved being a flyman, he felt called to something more.

Even though Mike was financially secure, he was smart in how he went about it by returning to school. First, he went to a junior college for his general education; then he transferred to Arizona State University. In addition to being awarded the Michael Colletto Scholarship, he told me that if he teaches two years, some of his tuition loans will be forgiven. "There are not enough students to take advantage of the program." While going to college, you can avoid racking up a huge debt. Mike said that although a lot of states have student loan forgiveness programs, it often involves a sacrifice; you may have to teach in a Title 1 or a remote school district. "There's really a need there, and it will reduce the cost." He wants to teach where there is the most need, anyway. He is passionate about helping others less fortunate. "So many people don't have the knowledge to help themselves or their children. Hopefully, we can empower future generations. This is something you don't lock up and not share."

Mike's also worked on the side to pay for college, so he doesn't decimate his savings. He says that it's much harder for his classmates sitting beside him at college. "Younger students have to work, study, and a lot of them are raising kids. I don't have the same situation, so in some ways it's easier to be an older student." Mike's wife also takes a class at a time and is doing it for fun. At her junior college, it's only $300 per class.

Even though Mike has been smart about his schooling, he is concerned about education in our society. He explained:

> I feel teachers are underpaid. In Arizona, in particular, teachers are not as well compensated. Most of the schools are funded by taxes, and people don't want to pay more taxes, but they want to take their most important commodity, the people who are going to take care of us in older age, and put them into close to a minimum-wage job. When people continually vote down initiatives for education, there is something wrong with our sense of value. We should be paying teachers what we pay doctors, not what we pay our dog walkers.
>
> The problem is the really qualified people will choose a better option. If they can make twice the money, with half the stress, how can they see teaching as a viable option? I understand nobody wants to pay more taxes, but there is a social responsibility where we owe it to our kids to educate them. I don't want to be taken care of by a bunch of morons. Education is what makes it happen.

Mike also feels it's important for parents to be engaged in their kids' education:

> Parents need to take more responsibility in educating their children. You can't just drop them off at school and put all the accountability on the educators. Parents need to go to schools and ask what should be taught. I'm going to be part of the solution. I'm going to be proactive. All parents want a better life for their children. I don't think all parents expect their kids to be millionaires, but they'd like their kids not to worry, not to care if their car breaks down. People want their kids to

feel safe and be able to pay their bills without worrying where their next paycheck is going to come from. And if parents want their kids to be able to do better, to do more, they need to be involved.

Mike and I talked about financial literacy, and the fact that it's not taught enough in schools. He told me we need to advocate for it, and he personally challenged me to be an advocate. I hope, through this book, you will be an advocate for yourself, and for those you love.

In closing, Mike shared the best nugget of wisdom—one I have been trying to teach throughout this book: "It's not teaching them about their finances so much but teaching them they don't need to settle. They can do more."

A Final Note

"The harder you work, the luckier you get."

— Gary Player

*I*T REALLY IS QUITE SIMPLE. Here is how to be conscious, present, and purposeful in your wealth:

- Explore your creativity in ways that are about the experiences, not the money or status.

- Judge yourself against yourself, not your neighbors, your friends, or your parents.

- Be cognizant of the messages and stories you make up for yourself about money.

- Plan for your best future by bucketing for the life you want.

- Don't live in debt.

- Have the right people around you to help and guide you.

- Keep your emotions in check. Is your feeling being triggered by something from your past?

- Plan for the best future for yourself, and your loved ones, too!

- Save.

- Be intentional in your spending.

- Change your attitude to the positive and explore how you can improve a few habits as a daily practice.

You deserve to be who you were meant to be. Money should help, not hold you back. You have one life. It seems so obvious: You need the basic necessities to live, and money is the main way to obtain those necessities. But beyond that, *you* can tap into the *joy* of living, by mastering your view of money, wealth, possessions, and the short time you have on this earth!

Money is much more than just paper in a wallet, numbers on a bank account statement, or a collection of things you bought on a bookcase. Money is a transfer of energy or power. Harness a view of abundance and your own inner strength; this will help you move forward.

I hope you start looking for the freedom to do and be whatever you want. You are never too old, and you are never too young, to make your life what you want it to be. It will take a clear focus and, like an athlete, practice.

I hope you find freedom to be with family and have relationships, not just work and go through the motions of waiting for a paycheck, collapsing into bed, waking up, working, and waiting for a paycheck.

Write down your goals and get a good handle on your wealth practices. If you don't know where to start, look for a financial planner who will truly listen and help you process what financial freedom means for you.

Now that you've read this book, how will your Money Messages and the stories you tell yourself about your reality and your future change? By understanding your history, your triggers, and your Money Messages, you will learn how to find healthy ways to grow in your story with money and get to know the type of investor or saver you are. I hope you have a handle on any self-sabotaging behavior within your story, and moving forward, you can gently stand up and say goodbye to the shadow that has sat beside you in the past.

I hope I have helped you see a new future that includes some new money and life messages that empower you. The tools in this book will help you identify and improve your story about wealth. You've read several stories you could learn from. If need be, go back and reread the book or the sections you need to work on. Then seek out other resources as well. I encourage you to be always looking for ways you can be more aware, awake, and conscious in your life, and be more awake in your choices about spending, saving, and pursuing your dreams.

You have one life. Live it fully and with presence.

BONUS SECTION
ADDITIONAL
MONEY MESSAGE TOOLS

Your Next Amazing Journey
in Reading

*I*F YOU ARE ANYTHING LIKE me, when you reach the end of a book, you may feel sad: "Is it over already? Where do I go next?" I'd like to point you to some of my favorite authors who have inspired me, cajoled me, and kicked me in the pants. Most books I "read" are audio books because I like to devour them as I commute. Some books, like *Small Fry* by Lisa Brennan-Jobs, give insight into one of the most brilliant minds in history, her dad Steve Jobs, and the pitfalls of avarice. Others inspire, like those of Wayne Dyer. Some are pure entertainment, like fiction writer Kristin Hannah, who explores, through storytelling, power, extreme wealth and poverty, and survival against all odds. And, okay conservative friends, yes, Barack Obama is on my list, but *The Audacity of Hope* is a *great* book. Like him or hate him, Obama offers a rare glimpse into a president's deepest thoughts before his time in office, and if you listen to the audio book, you will hear his own voice.

All the authors I mention here have made me think about my world, my lifestyle, and what wealth or poverty means. This is not to say I agree with their every single word, but all of them have made me *think*! So as not to play favorites, I have put my list in alphabetical order. I have listed my favorite work by each author or the book I think is the best introduction to that author, but many of these authors have written multiple books so I encourage you to explore them beyond what is listed here.

Maya Angelou. *I Know Why the Caged Bird Sings.*

Gabrielle Bernstein. *Awakening Your Authentic Power.*

Lisa Brennan-Jobs. *Small Fry.*

Brené Brown. *The Power of Vulnerability.*

Wayne Dyer. *Excuses Begone!*

Kristin Hannah. *The Great Alone.*

Rachel Hollis. *Girl, Wash Your Face.*

Susan R. Komives et al. *Leadership for a Better World.*

Margaret Magnussen. *The Gentle Art of Swedish Death Cleaning.*

Barack Obama. *The Audacity of Hope.*

Judith Orloff. *The Empath's Survival Guide.*

Karen Putz. *Unwrapping Your Passion.*

Jen Sincero. *You Are a Badass.*

Eckhart Tolle. *Enlightened Relationships.*

TED Talks

*I*T'S HARD FOR ME TO mention a single TED Talk that has most influenced me because I listen to them so often. I like the Pandora podcasts *TED Talks Daily*, and NPR's *TED Radio Hour*. I have also attended two TEDx Naperville conferences, and I enjoyed both. I would highly recommend finding your local TEDx and attending in person, if you have the chance. If there is not one in your community, consider starting a TEDx where you live! Learn more at: https://tinyurl.com/organizeTEDx.

If you are unfamiliar with TED Talks, according to an article by David Roos on Howstuffworks.com, the concept of bringing together the "best and brightest" to share ideas got its start in the idea hub of the Silicon Valley in 1984 by Richard Saul Wurman, before the World Wide Web even existed! It was not an immediate success, but as the purpose and format of the gathering evolved, it became a conference with a unique format of eighteen minutes per speaker specifically about Technology, Entertainment, and Design, thus the name TED. Today, the mission of "Ideas worth spreading" has impacted millions of people throughout the world. As of this writing, more than 100,000 TED Talks have been presented, over 30,000 events have been held, with viewership between live events and online video and audio replays in the hundreds of millions.

Below are a few TED Talks I have mentioned in this book or that have been pivotal in my journey of self-discovery:

Brené Brown's TED Talk, "Listening to Shame"
 https://www.ted.com/talks/brene_brown_listening_to_shame

Lori Gottlieb's TED Talk, "How Changing Your Story Can Change Your Life" www.tinyurl.com/LoriGottlieb

I found this talk fascinating because Gottlieb and I work in different professions, but we have come to many of the same conclusions independently. She focuses on your personal story, and it is worth the eighteen minutes it takes to listen to it.

AdaPia D'Errico's TED Talk, "Journey to Freedom, Her Story AdaPia"
 https://tinyurl.com/AdaPia

Amy Cuddy's TED Talk, "Your Body Language May Shape Who You Are" https://tinyurl.com/amycuddybodylanguage

Mel Robbins' TED Talk, "How to Stop Screwing Yourself Over"
 https://tinyurl.com/MelRobbinsUniqueness

How to Find a Financial Advisor

*M*ANY GOOD PEOPLE ARE IN financial services. However, the industry is so large that it can be hard to know where to turn when it comes to getting financial advice. What does it all mean, and what questions should you ask? I've simplified matters into an easy questionnaire you can use when you interview financial advisors. First, I'll explain the questions so you understand why they matter, and then I will repeat them with space for you to write answers when you interview a potential financial advisor.

What are your qualifications?

Licenses

Registered representatives, also called stockbrokers, investment representatives, and bank representatives, are paid commissions to sell investment and insurance products. Their primary sales licenses are Series 6 or Series 7.

The Series 63 is a securities license entitling the holder to solicit orders for any type of security in a particular state.

The Series 65 is a securities license required by most US states for individuals who act as investment advisors or financial advisors. The Series 65 exam, called the Uniform Investment Adviser Law Examination, covers laws, regulations, ethics, and topics such as retirement planning, portfolio management strategies, and fiduciary responsibilities. The Series 66 exam is a combination of Series 63 and Series 65, but since a prerequisite for taking the exam is successful completion of the Series 7 exam, it does not include the product, analysis, and strategy questions that are a large part of the Series 65 (which are already part of the 7).

Financial advisors who work for companies called Registered Investment Advisors (RIAs) are called Investment Advisor Representatives (IARs). They are compensated by a flat fee, an hourly fee, or a fee based on assets under management and are financial fiduciaries, so they are held to the highest ethical standards in the financial services industry.

Money managers have the same registrations and characteristics as financial advisors. Their distinguishing feature is that they make decisions for investors without their approval in advance.

Financial planners are a tough category. There are no licensing requirements for someone to call themselves a financial planner. Anyone can claim to be a financial planner, whether it is true or not. However, different certifications can signify a person's level of experience and expertise.

Certifications for Financial Planners

This is not an exhaustive list, but it includes the most common certifications financial planners will pursue to better assist their clients with their unique needs and goals.

Financial Planning Intermediate Level Certifications

AAMS Accredited Asset Management Specialist: Provides recommendations based on all aspects of a client's total financial picture. Has general certification for financial advisors on investments, insurance, tax, retirement, and estate planning.

AWMA Accredited Wealth Management Advisor: Addresses complex financial issues faced by affluent clients.

CDFA Certified Divorce Financial Analyst: Provides specialized training to accounting, financial, and legal professionals in the field of pre-divorce financial planning.

ADPA Accredited Domestic Partnership Advisor: Focuses on the unique needs of domestic partners, including LGBT and heterosexual couples who have chosen not to marry.

ChFC Chartered Financial Consultant (ChFC): Oversees financial planning needs of individuals, professionals, and small business owners, including insurance, income taxation, retirement planning, investments, and estate planning.

Financial Planning Advanced Level Certifications

CFP (Certified Financial Planner): A professional certification mark for financial planners conferred by the Certified Financial Planner Board of Standards (CFP Board) in the United States, and by twenty-five other organizations affiliated with Financial Planning Standards Board (FPSB), the international owner of the CFP mark outside of the United States. To receive authorization to use the designation, the candidate must meet education, examination, experience, and ethics requirements, and pay an ongoing certification fee.

CFA (Chartered Financial Analyst): The program covers a broad range of topics relating to investment management, financial analysis, stocks, bonds, and derivatives, and provides generalist knowledge of other areas of finance.

CPA/PFS (Certified Public Accountant with the Personal Financial Specialist Credential): CPA with the combination of tax expertise and knowledge of financial planning.

MBA in Finance (Master of Business Administration with a focus in finance): Finance degree programs at the master's level prepare you to assume roles of greater responsibility, including management and executive positions. An MBA in Finance does not necessarily prepare a person to be a financial planner, but in combination with other certifications, it shows a dedication to learning.

What experience do you have?

How many years of experience a person has is just as important as the letters behind their name. Someone who has had five, ten, or twenty years of hands-on experience "in the trenches" helping clients is just as, if not more important, than all the book smarts in the world.

Get to know the person. Think of it as a bit like a first date. This is a person you will be leaning on for advice, and who may be guiding you for years. Why did this financial planner get into the business? What are the financial planner's goals for the future of their business? If you need to reach them, what is their availability—what days, what hours? Do they charge each time you call, or will you have to talk to their assistant most of the time?

What services do you offer?

The services a financial planner offers will vary and depend on their credentials, areas of expertise, and the firm for which they work. Some planners offer financial planning advice on a range of topics but do not sell financial products; others provide advice in specific areas such as taxation. Ask the financial planner if they are a fiduciary. A fiduciary must act in the best interest of their clients. Anyone who cannot claim fiduciary status must disclose any conflicts of interest such as bonuses and special payouts for selling certain products or producing a certain volume of transactions, new assets brought to the firm, or gaining commissions for selling a product.

What is your approach to financial planning?

The types of services a financial planner will provide will vary. Some planners prefer to develop detailed financial plans encompassing all of a client's financial goals. Others choose to work in specific areas such as taxation, estate planning, insurance, and investments. Ask whether the individual deals only with clients with specific net worth and income levels, and whether the planner will help you implement the plan they develop or refer you to others who will do so. If you're keen to deal with a firm that puts real financial planning service at the heart of its service to clients, you will want to search out a firm that is a Registered Investment Advisor. The advisors working for these firms do not receive commissions for selling products, but rather a fee based on assets managed or on an hourly basis.

Will you be the only person working with me?

It is quite common for a financial planner to work with their team to provide the full financial planning service to you. You may want to meet everyone who will be working with you, which will often involve money managers, back office administration, and paraplanners. These professionals work to support the financial planner, providing technical research, backup, report writing, and analysis.

How will I pay for your services?

There is not, and never has been, such a thing as a free lunch, or free financial advice. Your planner should disclose in writing in advance the cost of their services and how they will charge you.

You will also want to find out other costs such as administrative or annual costs, money management costs, transaction costs, and security or fund internal costs (hidden expenses). *Every* investment will have costs in some aspect. (If someone tells you that you don't pay these costs at all, run!) Transparency and effort on the part of the financial planner to explain these costs, the value you are paying for, and what they will do to minimize expenses while still maintaining the quality you are looking for will guarantee a secure working relationship.

How much do you typically charge?

Although the amount you pay the planner depends on your particular needs, even at an early stage in the process, the financial planner should be able to provide you with an estimate of costs based on the work they will do for you.

How are you regulated?

In the United States, the main regulating bodies are the SEC, FINRA, and state insurance agencies (for investment representatives and financial advisors who also sell or advise on insurance).

To check if someone is a registered representative, stockbroker, investment representative, or bank representative, visit http://brokercheck.finra.org/

To check on investment advisors, visit http://www.adviserinfo.sec.gov/

How often do you review my situation?

Good financial planners will make sure they review your situation at least annually. Many will do so more frequently, but a thorough review once a year is sufficient to ensure your plan keeps up to date with your changing circumstances.

Can I have it in writing?

Finally, be sure to ask the planner to provide you with a written agreement that details the services that will be provided.

Questions to Ask a Financial Advisor

What are your qualifications?

_____

_____

_____

What experience do you have?

_____

_____

_____

What services do you offer?

_____

_____

_____

What is your approach to financial planning?

_____

_____

_____

Will you be the only person working with me?

_____

_____

_____

How will I pay for your services?

_____

_____

_____

How much do you typically charge?

_____

_____

_____

How are you regulated?

_____

_____

_____

How often do you review my situation?

_____

_____

_____

Can I have it in writing?

_____

_____

_____

Sources used to create this summary: Wikipedia, Investopedia, Forbes, The College for Financial Planning, SEC, FINRA, and CISI.

Savvy Money-Saving Food Prep Tips from Jody and Her Grandma

*O*NE EXAMPLE FOR MY FUTURE recipe book, coming straight from my farm Grandma, is to buy a whole turkey or chicken (versus the more expensive per pound chicken breasts or processed tenders), and use the bones to create a broth for soup. Split the cooked turkey or chicken up into multiple meals, like a casserole one night, fajitas one night, and chicken omelets the next morning.

There's no need to gorge an entire chicken in one meal and throw the rest away. A ½ cup of chopped chicken is about 3 ounces, which equals one serving. One pound of chicken (16 ounces) is about 2 cups of chopped chicken. (Sounding like a word problem from grade school?)

Pick the carcass after the meal for chicken salad sandwiches. I bet you can get at least 3-6 ounces of chicken off that carcass that you used to throw away. How much do you pay for a chicken salad sandwich at Panera? I've seen recipes so you can make your own "Panera Chicken Salad." You can get really fancy and throw in some grapes, celery, and dill relish. And then, any left-over chicken salad can go on top of a mixed greens salad.

I love to grow my own lettuce, garlic, tomatoes, peppers, jalapenos, and various herbs, and I grow them from seedlings...just like my grandma and my mom. Never learned how? There are classes all over the place, and YouTube is an amazing resource.

Just a few generations ago, when everything was farm to table, and there was no such thing as "fast food," nothing was wasted. I still remember, as a child, helping my family at the farm during butchering day, but I do draw the line at head cheese, chicken legs, and tripe. I was a "city girl" with particular tastes, and a bit of a brat. I would say "Eww" and "Gross" at a lot of things. I will never ever forget the image of my farm aunt Marion, complete with her sly smile after a day of butchering, frying up a chicken neck and leaning up against the counter, gnawing on it like it was a precious, rare delicacy.

As an aside, have you ever pondered the popularity of chicken wings? Did you know this phenomenon comes from poor people figuring out how to make what was once the "undesirable" part of a chicken good to eat? When I was a kid, chicken wings were super-cheap. Now, chicken wings are one of the more expensive meat products at the grocery store, just because they're popular. Why not cut off the wings before cooking your whole chicken and freeze them? When you've collected enough, have a home-spun wild wings night. Every couple of months, it can be a special treat, as it should be.

ABOUT THE AUTHORS

JODY ROBINSON IS A WEALTH manager with offices in Illinois. Jody's background covers the full scope of financial planning: wealth management, portfolio construction, insurance, estate and tax planning.

Jody understands the complexity of personal and financial situations. She specializes in helping individuals rewrite their Money Messages so they can create purposeful wealth.

She successfully faced the challenge of transitioning to an independent practice while working as a divorced parent. She has since remarried, and her expanded family includes her son, four adult stepchildren, and a giant, but gentle, black Labrador.

Jody actively participates in her local Rotary club and other volunteer activities, promoting youth leadership and humanitarian service. She is a past Assistant District Governor and Oak Forest Rotarian of the Year 2018. In 2011, she received the Zeke McIntyre Pioneer Award from a large financial corporation. The award recognizes excellence in new financial advisors.

For fun, Jody enjoys cooking, gardening, swimming, and listening to audiobooks. You can also find her out walking her dog or singing like a crazy woman while driving.

*K*AREN *P*UTZ IS KNOWN AS "The Passion Mentor." She is the author of multiple books, including *Unwrapping Your Passion, Creating the Life You Truly Want*, and *The Passion Path*. She has been featured on *The Today Show* and in *O, The Oprah Magazine*.

Karen, her husband, and three children are deaf. Their adorable Westie is also deaf.

For fun, Karen enjoys cooking, gardening, swimming, and reading books. You can also find her walking on water as a barefoot water skier.

Made in the USA
Columbia, SC
14 February 2020